BENNINGTON

POTTERY AND

PORCELAIN

A Guide to Identification

BY RICHARD CARTER BARRET

Halftone Photographs by Lloyd Oppenheimer

BONANZA BOOKS • NEW YORK

ACKNOWLEDGMENTS

Perhaps no other American-made items are as misunderstood, mistaken and unintentionally misrepresented as are the ceramic products produced at Bennington during the middle of the nineteenth century. It is my intention to show in this book the variety of the types of items and the types of wares which were made here. I have not included illustrations of every known piece manufactured, but I have made a sincere effort to illustrate every known type of ware and all of the most significant production items.

Such a volume as this is the result of the cooperation of many people. The generous assistance and gracious understanding of Mrs. Elizabeth McCullough Johnson (Mrs. Elmer H. Johnson), who gave me complete access to her unrivaled collection, actually made this book possible. My grateful appreciation is also given to the Trustees of Bennington Museum for the use of the John Spargo collection as well as numerous smaller collections in the Museum. Other institutions whose various staff members assisted me in research include The Brooklyn Museum, Brooklyn, N. Y.; The Metropolitan Museum of Art, New York City; The Smithsonian Institution, Washington, D. C.; The Wadsworth Athenaeum, Hartford, Connecticut.

Private individuals have been of great assistance in many instances. In addition to the owners of items illustrated who are listed elsewhere, I would especially like to express appreciation to George S. McKearin, Esq. and his daughters, Mrs. Helen McKearin Powers and Mrs. Betty McKearin Gruene for continued help in many ways and to my good friends George Abraham and Gilbert May, antiquarians extraordinary. I am grateful to Miss Helena Norton, Mrs. Isabel Norton Leonard, Mrs. Henry D. Fillmore and Mrs. Fanny Fenton Fillmore McKeon for use of family treasures and traditions. Important assistance has also been received from Mrs. Bartlett Arkell, Mr. and Mrs. Robert Bischoff, Channing Hare, Esq., Mr. Allen D. Hill, Mr. and Mrs. Robert Jacobs and Miss Marcia Riley.

To Lloyd Oppenheimer, who worked so hard and so long on the photography goes a major portion of the credit for the usefulness of this book. And my grateful appreciation to Walter Hard, Jr., editor of *Vermont Life,* for permission to use the excellent color photographs by John F. Smith, Jr.

And finally, to two staff members of Bennington Museum, Mrs. Harold G. Green and Mrs. James F. Pfleger, who have personally assisted me in solving the difficult and multiple problems of organization, continuity and composition of material, I give my sincerest personal gratitude.

It is my sincere desire that our combined efforts will bring proper recognition to Bennington for its important contribution to the manufacture of ceramics in America.

RICHARD CARTER BARRET

Old Bennington, Vermont

(F)

© MCMLVIII by Richard Carter Barret

Library of Congress Catalog Card Number: 58-8312

Printed in the United States of America

This edition published by Bonanza Books,
a division of Crown Publishers, Inc.

CONTENTS

ACKNOWLEDGMENTS ii

HALFTONE PHOTOGRAPH CREDITS iv

INTRODUCTION 2

SECTION I: FUNCTIONAL ITEMS

    Chapter One: Pitchers 22

    Chapter Two: Table Ware 82

    Chapter Three: Kitchen and Household Accessories 102

SECTION II: FANCY ARTICLES

    Chapter Four: Vases, Ewers, Cologne Bottles and Trinket Boxes 142

    Chapter Five: Statuettes and Figures 256

    Chapter Six: Animals and Birds 280

    Chapter Seven: Novelty Items 308

LIST OF ILLUSTRATIONS 343

INDEX OF ILLUSTRATIONS 346

HALFTONE PHOTOGRAPH CREDITS

The items illustrated in Figures and Plates not listed below are all from the magnificent collection of Elizabeth McCullough Johnson. Unless otherwise listed, all items in the same plate are from the collection indicated.

The following are the abbreviations used for ownership credits:

Bennington Museum Collections ....BM

Brooklyn Museum,
  Brooklyn, N. Y. ....BrM

Elizabeth McCullough Johnson
  Collection ....EMJ

John Spargo Collection,
  Bennington Museum ....JS

Pitken Collection, Wadsworth
  Athenaeum, Hartford, Conn. ....WA

Fig. V:JS; Fig. VII: Miss Helena Norton; Fig. IX:A—JS, B—EMJ, C—BM, D—Mr. and Mrs. Robert Bischoff; Fig. X:JS. Plates: 1:JS; 2:JS; 3:JS; 5:JS; 10:JS; 12: Mrs. Isabel Norton Leonard; 14:JS; 15:JS; 16: Mrs. Henry D. Fillmore; 18:BrM; 22:A—BM, B-C-D—JS; 26—A—BM, B—EMJ, C-D-E—JS; 27:A—BM, B-C—JS; 28:JS; 29:JS; 30:JS; 31:BM; 32:JS; 35:A—Mr. and Mrs. Harold Duckworth, B—Mr. and Mrs. Richard C. Barret; 36:A—BM, B—Mr. and Mrs. Richard C. Barret; 37:A—Mr. and Mrs. Richard C. Barret, B—JS, C—Mr. and Mrs. Richard C. Barret; 38:A —JS, B-EMJ; 40:JS; 44:A—EMJ, B—JS; 44A:A—EMJ, B—JS; 45: Mrs. Isabel Norton Leonard; 46:JS; 47:A—EMJ, B-C—BM; 49:A-B—JS, C—BM; 52:JS; 54:A—EMJ, B—BM; 55:BrM; 59:A—JS, B—EMJ; 60:JS; 61:JS; 63:WA; 65:A—JS, B—BM; 66:JS; 67:BM; 69:A—JS, B—EMJ; 70:JS; 74:A—BM, B—JS, C—BM, D—JS; 75:A—JS, B—BM; 76:BM; 77:WA; 78:JS; 79: Mr. and Mrs. Richard C. Barret; 80:BM; 83:BM; 85:BM; 86:BM; 87:JS; 89:BM; 91:JS; 92:JS; 98:WA; 99:JS; 101:JS; 105:A-B-C-D-E-JS, F-G-H—BM; 109:JS; 121:JS; 123:JS; 125:JS; 126:JS; 128:BM; 129:JS; 132:A—JS, B—BM, C—JS, D—BM, E—JS, F—BM, G—JS; 133:A-B-C—JS, D—BM, E-EMJ, F—JS; 135:JS; 136:JS; 137:BM; 138:JS; 139: Miss Ruth Hart Eddy; 144:JS; 147:A—BM, B—JS; 150:A-B-C—BM, D—EMJ; 151:JS; 154:A—JS, B—Mrs. Isabel Norton Leonard, C—JS; 160:JS; 161:JS; 163:JS; 165:JS; 166:WA; 167:JS; 168:BM; 169:JS; 170:JS; 171:JS; 172:JS; 173:JS; 174:JS; 175:JS; 176:BM; 177:BM; 178:JS; 179:JS; 180:JS; 181:JS; 184:JS; 185:A—JS, B—BM, C—Mr. and Mrs. Robert Bischoff, D-E—JS; 187:A—BM, B—JS; 189:JS; 191:BM; 193:WA; 196:JS; 197:JS; 199:JS; 200:JS; 203:JS; 204:JS; 205:WA; 210:WA; 211:WA;

215:JS; 218:A-B—BM, C-D—EMJ; 232-A —EMJ, B—Miss Ruth Hart Eddy, C—EMJ, D-E-F—Channing Hare, Esq; 240:JS; 253:JS; 254:JS; 295: General and Mrs. Francis Englehart; 296:BM; 301:JS; 305:BM; 318:A — Channing Hare, Esq., B—Miss Ruth Hart Eddy; 335:BM; 340: Channing Hare, Esq.; 341:JS; 343: Mrs. Earle Whittaker; 344:A—JS, B—BM; 346:JS; 347:BM; 354:A—JS, B—BM, C-D-E-F—JS; 355:A—Mrs. John Sloane, B—BM; 357:JS; 358:JS; 359:JS; 360:WA; 362:JS; 363:WA; 368:JS; 372:JS; 374:BM; 375:BM; 380:JS; 381:JS; 382:A—EMJ, B—BM; 384:WA; 388:JS; 397:JS; 398:WA; 403:JS; 404:A-B—BM, C—JS, D—Mr. and Mrs. R. T. Bixler; 405:JS; 408:A—JS, B—EMJ; 409:BM; 409A:BM; 411:JS; 413:JS; 414:JS; 415:JS; 416:A—JS, B—EMJ, C—BM, D-E—JS; 416A: same as 416; 418:JS; 419:A—JS, B-C—BM; 420:BM; 423:WA; 427:WA; 429:JS; 430:JS; 433:JS; 435: Channing Hare, Esq.; 447:JS; 449:A—Mrs. Isabel Norton Leonard, B-C—JS.

PHOTOGRAPH CREDITS LISTED BY OWNERSHIP

ELIZABETH McCULLOUGH JOHNSON COLLECTION:

Fig. I; Fig. II; Fig. III; Fig. IV; Fig. VI; Fig. VIII; Fig. IX—B; Fig. XI; Fig XII. Plates: 4; 6; 7; 8; 9; 11; 13; 17; 19; 20; 21; 23; 24; 25; 26—B; 33; 34; 38—B; 39; 41; 42; 43; 44—A; 44A—A; 47—A; 48; 50; 51; 53; 54—A; 56; 57; 58; 59—B; 62; 64; 68; 69—B; 71; 72; 73; 81; 82; 84; 88; 90; 93; 94; 95; 96; 97; 100; 102; 103; 104; 106; 107; 108; 110; 111; 112; 113; 114; 115; 116; 117; 118; 119; 120; 122; 124; 127; 130; 131; 133—E; 134; 140; 141; 142; 143; 145; 146; 148; 149; 150—D; 152; 153; 155; 156; 157; 158; 159; 162; 164; 182; 183; 186; 188; 190; 192; 194; 195; 198; 201; 202; 206; 207; 208; 209; 212; 213; 214; 216; 217; 218—C-D; 219; 220; 221; 222; 223; 224; 225; 226; 227; 228; 229; 230; 231; 232—A-C; 233; 234; 235; 236; 237; 238; 239; 241; 242; 243; 244; 245; 246; 247; 248; 249; 250; 251; 252; 255; 256; 257; 258; 259; 260; 261; 262; 263; 264; 265; 266; 267; 268; 269; 270; 271; 272; 273; 274; 275; 276; 277; 278; 279; 280; 281; 282; 283; 284; 285; 286; 287; 288; 289; 290; 291; 292; 293; 294; 297; 298; 299; 300; 302; 303; 304; 306; 307; 308; 310; 311; 312; 313; 314; 315; 316; 317; 319; 320; 321; 322; 323; 324; 325; 326; 327; 328; 329; 330; 331; 332; 333; 334; 336; 337; 338; 339; 342; 345; 348; 349; 350; 351; 352; 353; 356; 361; 364; 365; 366; 367; 369; 370; 371; 373; 376; 377; 378;

379; 382—A; 383; 385; 386; 387; 389; 390; 391; 392; 393; 394; 395; 396; 399; 400; 401; 402; 406; 407; 408—B; 410; 412; 416—B; 416A—B; 417; 421; 422; 424; 425; 426; 428; 431; 432; 434; 436; 437; 438; 439; 440; 441; 442; 443; 444; 445; 446; 448; 450.

JOHN SPARGO COLLECTION, BENNINGTON MUSEUM:

Fig. V; Fig. IX—A; Fig. X. Plates: 1; 2; 3; 5; 10; 14; 15; 22—B-C-D; 26—C-D-E; 27—B-C; 28; 30; 32; 37—B; 38—A; 40; 44—B; 44A—B; 46; 49—A-B; 52; 59—A; 60; 61; 65—A; 66; 69—A; 70; 74—B-D; 75—A; 78; 87; 91; 92; 99; 101; 105—A-B-C-D-E; 109; 121; 123; 125; 126; 129; 132—A-C-E-G; 133—A-B-C-F; 135; 136; 138; 144; 147—B; 151; 154—A-C; 160; 161; 163; 165; 167; 169; 170; 171; 172; 173; 174; 175; 178; 179; 180; 181; 184; 185—A-D-E; 187—B; 189; 196; 197; 199; 200; 203; 204; 215; 240; 253; 254; 301; 341; 344—A; 346; 354—A-C-D-E-F; 357; 358; 359; 362; 368; 372; 380; 381; 388; 397; 403; 404—C; 405; 408—A; 411; 413; 414; 415; 416—A-D-E; 416A—A-D-E; 418; 419—A; 429; 430; 433; 447; 449—B-C.

BENNINGTON MUSEUM COLLECTIONS:

Fig. IX—C. Plates: 22—A; 26—A; 27—A; 29; 31; 36—A; 47—B-C; 49—C; 54—B; 65—B; 67; 74—A-C; 75—B; 76; 80; 83; 85; 86; 89; 105—F-G-H; 128; 132—B-D-F; 133—D; 137; 147—A; 150—A-B-C; 168; 176; 177; 185—B; 187—A; 191; 218—A-B; 296; 305; 335; 344—B; 347; 354—B; 355—B; 374; 375; 382—B; 404—A-B; 409; 409A; 416—C; 416A—C; 419—B-C; 420.

PITKEN COLLECTION, WADSWORTH ATHENAEUM, HARTFORD, CONNECTICUT:

Plates: 63; 77; 98; 166; 193; 205; 210; 211; 360; 363; 384; 398; 423; 427.

INDIVIDUAL OWNERS

Mr. and Mrs. Richard C. Barret: 35—B; 36—B; 37—A-C; 79. Mr. and Mrs. Robert Bischoff: Fig. IX—D; 185—C. Mr. and Mrs. R. T. Bixler: 404—D. Brooklyn Museum, Brooklyn, N. Y.: 18; 55. Mr. and Mrs. Harold Duckworth: 35—A. Miss Ruth Hart Eddy: 139; 232—B; 318—B. General and Mrs. Francis A. Englehart: 295. Mrs. Henry D. Fillmore: 16. Channing Hare, Esq.: 232—D-E-F; 318—A; 340; 435. Mrs. Isabel Norton Leonard: 12; 45; 154—B; 449—A. Miss Helena Norton: Fig. VIII. Mrs. John Sloane: 355—A. Mrs. Earle Whittaker: 343.

BENNINGTON
POTTERY AND
PORCELAIN

——•——

BENNINGTON POTTERY AND PORCELAIN

A Guide to Identification

THE BENNINGTON POTTERIES

For collectors who have long sought a reliable aid to identification of the various ceramic articles known generally as "Bennington ware," the first guidepost is the fact that there were not one but two well known potteries which flourished in the town of Bennington, Vermont, during the mid-nineteenth century. These firms produced items in more than a dozen different types of pottery and porcelain. This very variety was its most important influence on American ceramic manufacture.

To trace their histories in detail would be outside the province of this volume, which is intended as a guide in determining the authenticity of pieces made in Bennington. (For a fuller historical survey the collector may wish to consult John Spargo's *Potters and Potteries of Bennington,* published in 1926 by *Antiques Magazine.*)

The first (and longest-lived) pottery works was created in Bennington by Captain John Norton in 1793, two years after Vermont became a state. It produced the simple wares required by the community—jugs, crocks, milk pans, plates, etc. For 101 years it was to be owned and operated by succeeding generations of Nortons. The other noted Bennington firm, which did not begin independent operation until about 1847, was directed during its prime by Christopher Webber Fenton, who was related by marriage to the son of the founder of the Norton pottery. There was a brief merger, which lasted only two years, 1845-1847.

The first examples known to have survived from the time Captain John Norton operated his kiln are made of redware covered with a thin clay slip or lead-glazed. Powdered lead was dusted on a piece which, when fired, melted and fused with the silica in the clay to form a hard, transparent glaze.

Salt-glazed gray stoneware items were produced soon after the early redware items. The first known marked examples of this type of ware were made from 1823-1828. These stoneware articles, which were usually marked with the Norton name, are more readily identifiable as Bennington-made than the unmarked redware.

To make this light gray or buff pottery, common salt was shoveled into the fire of the kiln. The salt vapors condensed on the pottery to form a thin, hard, highly acid-resistant finish. Articles were also glazed with a slip of tan, brown or black. The dark brown glaze was commonly used for kitchen wares, pitchers, batter jugs and mixing bowls.

Some examples of early stoneware are decorated with incised patterns or by designs in blue or brown slip which have been brushed on. Occasionally cobalt-blue swashes were applied around the handles or all across the design. Motifs such as flowers, birds, deer and vines were frequently employed in decoration. The best examples were produced from 1840 to 1860. Special pieces were made to commemorate an occasion or honor. These presentation stoneware jugs are considered rare.

Captain John Norton's pottery prospered and he took his eldest son Luman into partnership with him about 1812. Soon afterward

NOTE: *Except for the few comparison pieces made by other potteries, the halftone plates (Plates 1 to 450) and the color plates (Plates A to G) illustrate authenticated Bennington-made articles. Figures I to XII are items such as price-lists, marks and other related material.*

PLATE 1. OMINIDIA GERRY JUG. Named for its original owner, this is the earliest known authenticated piece of Bennington-made pottery. Known to have been made by Captain John Norton, not later than 1798, and probably somewhat earlier, but not before 1793. Red earthenware, covered with brown slip, with wavy incised band near top, both sides decorated with a spray of leaves in a lighter-colored slip, 6″ high.

PLATE 2. EARLY NORTON POTTERY PIECES. 1795-1800. These two pieces are among the earliest pieces known to have been made by Bennington's pioneer potter, Captain John Norton. A. Dark brown lead-glazed jug, 8¾″ high; B. Gray-brown footed vase, 7⅞″ high.

3

PLATE 4. BROWN SLIP-COVERED STONEWARE COVERED JAR. 1841-1861. Made for personal use of Julius Norton, head of the Norton potteries from 1841 to 1861. Yellow clay body, design incised through slip covering, only known example, 7¾" high.

PLATE 3. EARLY REDWARE JAR. One of the earliest pieces known. Made at Captain John Norton's pottery no later than 1800, dark reddish-brown high glaze, crude smoky blotch decorations, 9½" high. This type of early pottery cannot be attributed to Bennington without documentation or factual family history.

4

PLATE 5. NORTON STONEWARE JUG AND CROCKS. A. 1830-1835, extremely rare example with incised design partially filled with cobalt, marked with the owner's name "I. Judd," 17¾" high; B. 1823-1828. Extremely rare umber decoration with earliest of all Norton marks, "L. Norton & Co.," 9¾" high; C. 1850-1859, uncommon deer design in cobalt, marked "J. E. Norton," 13¼" high.

PLATE 6. NORTON STONEWARE JUGS AND PITCHER. *Top row:* A. Extremely rare handled jug, marked with owner's name, "T. Davis, Bennington," 12" high to handle, 28½" circ. *Bottom row:* B. Jug, bird decoration in cobalt, 1859-1861, marked "J. & E. Norton," 14½" high; C. Pitcher, cobalt design, 1859-1861, marked "J. & E. Norton," 13¼" high.

PLATE 7. Extremely Rare Stoneware Covered and Footed Bowl. Cobalt decoration, 4⅛" high. Incised design identical with marked piece below. This probably is also of the same date, 1847-1850.

PLATE 8. Extremely Rare Stoneware Jug with Applied Eagle. 1847-1850. Eagle is decorated with cobalt, holding an oval in which is incised owner's name, "A. Hathaway." Norton mark "Julius Norton" on reverse side, 4-gallon size, 18" high.

6

PLATE 9. NORTON STONEWARE CROCKS. 1850-1859. Both crocks marked "J. & E. Norton." A. Uncommon eagle design in cobalt, 3-gallon size, 13" high, 33" circ.; B. Extremely rare lion caricature, 4-gallon size, 11¼" high, 12" diam.

PLATE 10. ELABORATE STONEWARE WATER COOLER. Made for use in lobby of Hotel Putnam, Bennington, by J. & E. Norton, 1850-1859. Unique landscape of deer, trees, houses and elaborate bandings, all in cobalt, holes for four spigots at bottom and removable cover for ice at top, 33½" high.

PLATE 11. ELABORATE COBALT-DECORATED STONEWARE JUG. 1859-1861. Conventional flowers in basket design, with script name "James A. Gregg" at bottom, marked "J. & E. Norton," 9-gallon size, 23" high, 44" circ.

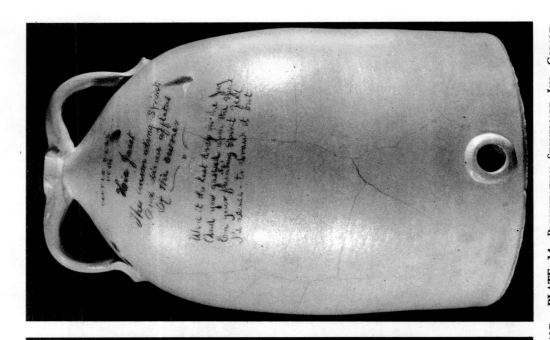

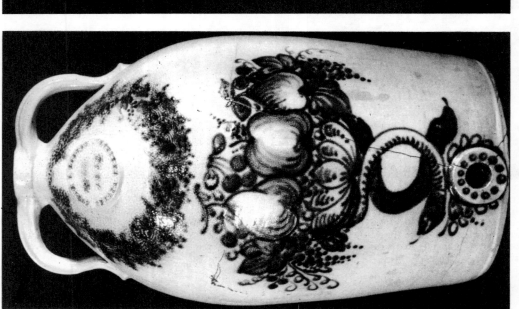

PLATE 12. PRESENTATION STONEWARE JUG, COBALT DECORATION. 1859. Unique piece made for Luman P. Norton. Applied circle at top has his name impressed, also "12 galls, 1859, IN VINO VERITAS," elaborate cobalt decoration, 26" high, 12" diam., at base. Such presentation jugs were extremely difficult pieces to make and fire without sagging or distortion.

PLATE 13. PRESENTATION STONEWARE JUG, COBALT DECORATION. 1864. Unique piece made for Calvin Park upon the occasion of his election to the Vermont State Legislature. Applied circle at top has his name impressed, also "Member from Woodford, 1864," cobalt horse signed "George J.," 23" high.

PLATE 14. PRESENTATION STONEWARE JUG, COBALT DECORATION. 1864. Made for Calvin Park, one of the partners in the Fenton pottery for a short while, upon the occasion of his election to the Vermont State Legislature. His name impressed, together with the date "1864," and a humorous poem, incised and filled with cobalt, 27" high.

another son, John, joined the firm. In 1823 the elder Norton handed over the pottery business to his two sons. From 1823 to 1827 their partnership was known as L. Norton & Company, but after 1828 Luman Norton managed the firm alone. The company turned out a variety of utilitarian stoneware jugs, preserve and butter pots, crocks and churns, all of which were straightforward and functional in design, with simple but pleasing decoration.

By the time L. Norton & Company moved to a new building in East Bennington (about 1833), John, Jr. had relinquished his interest in the pottery to Luman, who subsequently turned over most of the management of the business to his son Julius and finally retired in 1841. By this time Luman had acquired a potter son-in-law who was interested in making more decorative items.

About 1845 Julius Norton formed a partnership with his brother-in-law, Christopher Webber Fenton, but their association lasted only until 1847. Although Fenton, who liked to experiment, sought to expand the types of ceramic products offered by adding items in the new Parian ware popular in England, the long-established Norton firm steadily continued its output of homely stoneware and other crockery items. Fenton was able, however, to persuade Julius Norton to add to the stoneware items other articles made in a mottled glazed ware called Rockingham and in yellow and white glazed ware.

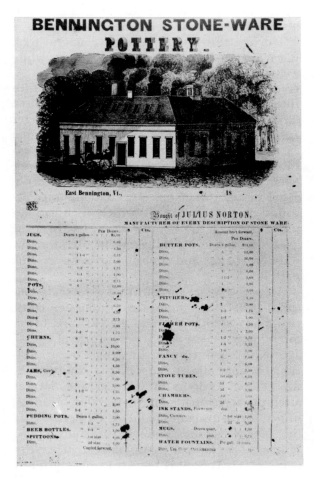

FIGURE I. PRICE LIST OF NORTON POTTERY. Use of name "Julius Norton" indicates it is a production list of the period 1847-1850. Interesting cut of Norton Pottery.

FIGURE II. PRICE LIST FROM NORTON & FENTON POTTERY, dated February 10, 1845, shows the limited variety and lack of decorative items produced during the period of the Norton-Fenton partnership.

By 1847 Bennington could boast two potteries, since Fenton had started a factory of his own in the north wing of the Norton pottery works, where he could continue his experiments in the new porcelain wares. There he strove to reproduce many popular English designs, particularly Staffordshire models, but he also produced items in Rockingham, yellow and white ware. He later moved his factory to another building and acquired two new partners, Alanson P. Lyman and Calvin Park. They advertised "Rockingham, white

flint and white earthen crockery ware" under the name of Lyman, Fenton & Park in April, 1848, although no marked pieces from this period have been found. Calvin Park withdrew from the company in 1849 and the firm then became known as Lyman, Fenton & Co. Many pieces bear the imprint of this partnership.

This volume is mainly concerned with the products made by the Fenton-directed pottery firm during the years from 1847 to 1858, when the company finally collapsed. This 11-year period produced a remarkably rich array of ceramic pieces, including many unusual articles made in Parian and in blue and white porcelain. An English designer, Daniel Greatbach, was responsible for many of the unusual animal designs and toby forms, most of which were produced in Rockingham and in a ware known as flint enamel.

During the 1850's several changes took place in the Fenton firm name. For a while Fenton's firm was managed by Oliver A. Gager, though Fenton retained a one-fifth interest. A new factory building, with three large kilns, went up in 1850. In 1853 Gager exhibited sample wares under the name "United States Pottery Company" at an exhibition held at the Crystal Palace in New York City. The pottery was later officially incorporated under this name. (A contemporary account of the exposition which included an illustration of the Fenton wares has been of great assistance to collectors of Bennington ware in dating and identifying items of this period.)

After five years of continuing financial instability because of increased production costs, rising prices of cordwood needed for firing the kilns as well as a high percentage of breakage incurred during packing and transportation by horse-drawn wagon, the company finally closed its doors on May 15, 1858. Several attempts were made to revive the business, under the firm names of A. A. Gilbert & Co., the New England Pottery Co. and T. A. Hutchins & Company. An individual by the name of H. Dewey is known to have ground feldspar at the site, but there is no record of any pottery being produced by him. The last dated piece known, a cuspidor, bears the date

FIGURE III. PRICE LIST OF FENTON'S POTTERY, dated July 20, 1852, has confirmed the authenticity of many articles. Many of the items listed have not yet been discovered.

10

1861. In 1870 the pottery buildings were torn down and a school was erected on the site.

During the 1850's the two Bennington potteries were producing a wide variety of similar wares. After 1850 Julius Norton and Edward Norton managed the older stoneware factory under the name of J. & E. Norton. They did make a few household items in Rockingham ware, notably the hound-handled pitchers (advertised in 1867 as "dog-handled pitchers"), but the Rockingham and flint enamel "fancy articles" and the Parian vases and figures were major production items of the Fenton-directed factory.

Norton stoneware items produced from 1859 to 1861 were marked "J. & E. Norton & Co." After the death of Julius Norton, the firm's order forms and letterheads showed his two sons, E. & L. P. Norton (Edward and Luman Preston Norton) as "manufacturers of every description of stone-ware." For two years (from 1881 to 1883) the firm was known simply as E. Norton. Edward Lincoln Norton carried on the business from 1883 to 1894.

FIGURE IV. ILLUSTRATED PRICE LIST OF J. & E. NORTON POTTERY, dated April, 1858, shows the selection of jugs and pots available from J. & E. Norton, "manufacturers of every description of stone-ware."

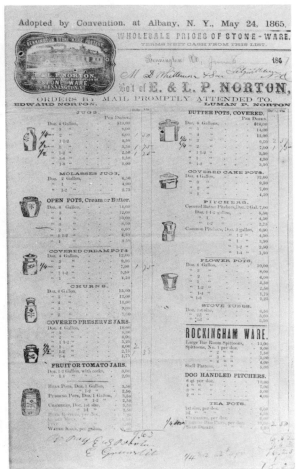

FIGURE V. PRICE LIST OF E. & L. P. NORTON POTTERY, dated June 8, 1867, is of particular interest because of the "Dog-Handled Pitchers" made in four sizes of Rockingham ware. This shows that the hound-handled pitchers were in production as late as 1867.

11

FIGURE VI. NORTON POTTERS, 1866. *Top row, left to right:* Frederick Godfrey, John H. Norton, Charles C. Kimball, J. A. N. Williams, William Bates. *Bottom row, left to right:* Jacob Metz, Edward H. Moore, William Smith, Frank H. Greenslet, Edward Norton (in top hat), Gilbert F. Burt, Jerome Johnson.

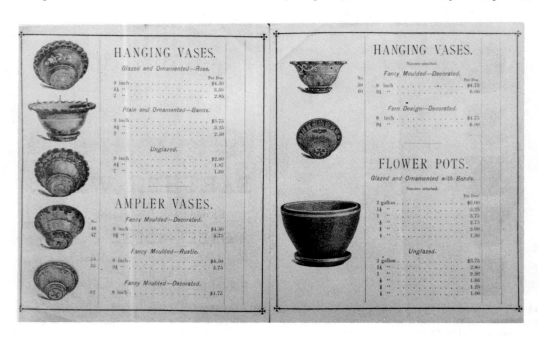

FIGURE VII. CATALOGUE PAGES FROM EDWARD NORTON & CO. POTTERY. 1883-1894. These seven hanging vases were sometimes made in imitation majolica, as well as brown slip-covered stoneware. (See also Pl. 191.)

FIGURE VIII. BENNINGTON LEADERS IN FLINT ENAMEL AND ROCKINGHAM PICTURE FRAMES. 1849-1858. *Top row:* A. Portrait of Julius Norton, flint enamel, 6″ high, 5½″ wide; B. Portrait of Judge Luman Norton, flint enamel, rococo, 11″ high, 9½″ wide; C. Portrait of Christopher Webber Fenton, flint enamel, 6″ high, 5½″ wide. *Bottom row:* D. Portrait of Edward Norton, Rockingham, oval, 5″ high, 4½″ wide; E. Unidentified woman, Rockingham, 3¼″ high, 3″ wide; F. U. S. Pottery Company factory, drawn by William Leake, the last of the Bennington potters, Rockingham, 11¾″ high, 10½″ wide; G. Portrait of Calvin Park, Rockingham, 7⅞″ high, 6⅝″ wide. (See also Pl. 204.)

A GUIDE TO MARKS

A chronological list of the various Norton Pottery markings, compiled by John Spargo and published in *Potters and Potteries of Bennington*, has proved valuable in dating Norton-made items. Note the slight variations through the years in the use of the "&" and "Co." or "Company." Of all the Norton marks, the one used between the years 1861 and 1881 (E. & L. P. Norton, Bennington, Vt.) is the most common.

Mark Used	*Period*
L. Norton & Co., Bennington, Vt.	1823-1828
L. Norton, Bennington, Vt.	1828-1833
L. Norton & Son, Bennington, Vt.	1833-1840
L. Norton & Son, East Bennington, Vt.	"
Julius Norton, Bennington, Vt.	1841-1845
Julius Norton, East Bennington, Vt.	"
J. Norton, East Bennington, Vt.	"
Norton & Fenton, Bennington, Vt.	1845-1847
Norton & Fenton, East Bennington, Vt.	"

Julius Norton, Bennington, Vt.	1847-1850
J. Norton, Bennington, Vt.	"
J. & E. Norton, Bennington, Vt.	1850-1859
J. Norton & Co., Bennington, Vt.	1859-1861
J. & E. Norton & Co., Bennington, Vt.	"
E. & L. P. Norton, Bennington, Vt.	1861-1881
E. Norton, Bennington, Vt.	1881-1883
Edward Norton, Bennington, Vt.	1883-1894
Edward Norton & Co., Bennington, Vt.	"
Edward Norton & Company, Bennington, Vt.	"
E. Norton & Co., Bennington, Vt.	"
Edward Norton Company, Bennington, Vt.	1886-1894

Only about one-fifth of the production of Fenton's pottery works was marked in any way. Eight separate marks, in addition to the two marks from the period of the Norton-Fenton partnership, are known to have been used by Fenton. (See Figures IX and X.) Some of these have had to be reproduced here in line drawings, since the only known examples are so filled with glaze that a clear photograph is impossible. The small circular mark has been found on only five examples. Care has been taken to reproduce exactly the crude, irregular lettering.

FIGURE IX. MARKS USED BY FENTON ON FLINT ENAMEL WARE. *Top row:* A. Most common mark, frequently appearing also on Rockingham and on two known Parian pieces. Used 1849-1858. B. Extremely rare mark, town name of Bennington does not appear. Used 1849-1858. *Bottom row:* C. Rare small 1849 mark. Used 1849-1858; D. Extremely rare mark, small. Used 1849-1858. Marks B and D have never been previously recorded or published.

FIGURE X. MARKS USED BY FENTON AND HIS POTTERY. *Top row:* E. Fenton's Works mark, 1845-1847. Used mainly on Parian ware, one known piece of scroddled ware and Rockingham. This mark was copied from similar design of Jones and Walley, Cobridge, England. F. U. S. Pottery Company "ribbon" mark, 1852-1858. Mainly used on Parian and blue and white porcelain, only very rarely on Rockingham and graniteware. *Bottom row:* G. U. S. Pottery Company "lozenge" mark, 1852-1858. Mainly used on Parian ware and smear-glazed porcelain. H. U. S. Pottery Company "oval" mark, 1853-1858. Mainly used on scroddled ware, rarely on Rockingham and flint enamel.

14

RECOGNIZING BENNINGTON WARE

In assessing the tremendous combined output of the two Bennington potteries one is continually amazed by the multiplicity of items they produced. One cannot simply call a piece a "Bennington pitcher" or a "Bennington bowl," since pitchers, bowls, and hundreds of assorted items in a number of patterns were produced by both factories in many materials and colors, among which the familiar examples with a brown tortoiseshell mottled glaze are only a small part.

The various wares include redware, glazed and unglazed; stoneware, salt-glazed and slip-covered; Rockingham, mottled and solid-color; flint enamel; scroddled ware; graniteware, plain glazed white or with gold and colored decoration; common white; common yellow; mortar ware; Parian porcelain, plain, unglazed; Parian body with applied colored decoration; white porcelain, highly glazed, smear-glazed, soft-paste and hard-paste; and colored porcelains, blue and white, tan and white, pink and white and green and white.

In order to attribute a particular item to Bennington, much more must be taken into account than just its color or material. For that reason several comparison pieces made by other potteries have been included in various sections where they are relevant. Of course capsule information on points of differentiation can never replace actual experience in learning to recognize details of design and manufacture.

At the Bennington Museum one of the popular exhibits is a display comparing similar patterns from different potteries. It is easy to be deceived on occasion if one uses pattern alone as the deciding factor in making an attribution. Often one cannot depend on pattern or glaze for assistance in reaching a decision. For example, the famous Bennington hound-handled pitchers were the forerunners of several American variations. The design was still being copied as late as 1900 by a pottery in Ohio.

In this book there has been no attempt made to indicate a definitive price guide, since each individual piece of Bennington ware has variations which affect the value to some extent. There are also differences in price in various shops and in various areas. Rockingham or flint enamel pie plates may be purchased in one shop, for example, for as little as $7.50, while in another shop, which may specialize in marked examples, the asking price may range from $65.00 to $85.00, depending on richness in coloring. Among the coveted animal figures sought by collectors, Bennington poodles with baskets of fruit or flowers have sold for anywhere from $350.00 to $1,000.00 a pair. Cow creamers vary in price today from $35.00 to $500.00 and toby bottles range from $50.00 to $450.00. The Bennington Museum has paid as much as $1,500.00 for a pair of grape-decorated blue and white porcelain ewers, yet it is possible to purchase pairs of the same pattern for as little as $50.00.

When pieces are added to the Bennington Museum collection they cease, of course, to have a financial value, since they are withdrawn from the market and are no longer for sale. It is difficult in any case to attempt to set standard values on Bennington ware items.

FIGURE XI. WOODCUT ILLUSTRATION OF CRYSTAL PALACE EXHIBIT. From *Gleason's Pictorial,* October 22, 1853. This illustration has been helpful in identifying Bennington-made items, some of which have never been located. See standing stag and doe at top right, clock case lower left.

15

A financial value is established by rival buyers who want the same piece, which may be up for sale at an auction. Even though a particular sum may be paid for an article, this does not serve as a true indication of its value in an open market. The purchaser may on occasion pay in part for a dealer's reputation and the assurance that if he is not satisfied with his purchase an equitable settlement will be made.

For the new Bennington ware collector an introductory "gallery" of items made for a special exhibition in New York in 1853 will serve to show the range of items produced at Bennington. Several items were made expressly for display and cannot be considered as standard production items, but the contemporary woodcut illustration demonstrates the variety of functional and ornamental articles on the market at the time.

A monumental structure made for the exhibition still stands in Bennington. The structure, said to have been modeled by Daniel Greatbach of England, is composed of four

PLATE 15. PARIAN STATUE AND STATUETTES. A. Large statue (30½″ high) was made to top monument at the 1853 Crystal Palace Exhibition at New York. Spoiled in the firing, it was discarded, and replaced by Pl. 16. The two small statuettes of "Praying Samuel" (4¾″ high) are shown to give scale.

PLATE 16. FAMOUS CENTRAL MONUMENT EXHIBITED IN NEW YORK, 1853. Made for the New York Crystal Palace Exhibition, this monumental piece is over ten feet high. This monument has remained for over 100 years on the porch of the double house once occupied by Judge Norton and his son-in-law, C. W. Fenton.

16

sections. Topping the monument was a Parian statuette of a woman and child. Parian figures, introduced by Fenton, gained him a name as the first American to produce this fine porcelain material.

Collectors today are especially interested in the "Fancy Articles," as they were once called, particularly the novelty items made in Rockingham ware, flint enamel, Parian and colored porcelains. Many of the handsome animal pieces made in the 1850's are now in the category of museum pieces.

BENNINGTON WARES

Since the early-rooted tradition of Bennington-made wares lies in the field of functional items—pitchers, tea sets, dishes, bowls, toilet sets and a wide miscellany of household items

PLATE 17. FAMOUS FLINT ENAMEL STANDING STAG. 1852. Only known example of the stag standing up. Known to have been exhibited at the 1853 Crystal Palace Exhibition in New York City. There was also a standing doe which has never been discovered. Both of these two standing deer were illustrated in *Gleason's Pictorial* (See Fig. XI and Pls. 364, 365 and 366.)

PLATE 18. FLINT ENAMEL APOSTLE PATTERN WATER COOLER. 1852-1853. Only known example. Eight apostles are separated by Doric columns. Made for 1853 Crystal Palace Exhibition in N. Y., this design is attributed to Daniel Greatbach. In addition to 1849 mark A, this piece is inscribed, in block letters on frieze of entablature: "Fenton's Enamel Patented 1849. Lyman, Fenton & Co., Manufacturers, Bennington, Vermont." 23½" high, 12¼" base width.

PLATE 19. PARIAN CLOCK CASE. 1852. Only known example, made for 1853 Crystal Palace Exhibition, 12½" high. (See Fig. XI.)

PLATE 20. EXTREMELY RARE PARIAN FLOWER CENTERPIECE. 1853. Only known example, made for 1853 Crystal Palace Exhibition, 6½" high, 12" long.

in constant daily use—these more homely pieces are discussed first in this book. Later chapters will take up what may be considered as "Fancy Articles," as they were called on the early price lists. These include primarily decorative and ornamental objects, although many of these, too, had functional uses. Toby jars contained snuff, cow creamers held cream, greyhounds formed inkwells and a fanciful figure might be combined with a holder for spills to light fires, pipes or lamps.

The decorative items made at Bennington were largely the products of the Fenton-directed pottery. Insofar as is known the Norton Potteries did not produce ornamented vases of any kind, but Christopher Webber Fenton, aided by English craftsmen, broke away from the older stoneware tradition and introduced many lovely pieces in Parian and blue and white porcelain in the 1850's. Ben-

nington-made items soon joined the tide of foreign-made decorative articles that cluttered Victorian mantels, parlor tables, whatnot shelves and dresser tops.

The brown glazed pottery from which many household items were made is known as Rockingham. This type of ware was first produced in Swinton, England, at the private pottery owned by the Marquis of Rockingham. Also made there, and known today as Rockingham, were fine porcelain tea sets in many designs. In America, however, Rockingham generally denotes a coarse ware with a brown tortoiseshell mottled glaze. Articles made in early Rockingham ware were sometimes called "dark luster." The solid brown Rockingham was not produced in as large quantity as the mottled type.

This mottled brown Rockingham is to pottery what gabardine is to textiles. From about 1835 on every sizable pottery in America has produced Rockingham. Thus a piece of pottery can be Bennington-made Rockingham, East Liverpool, Ohio, Rockingham or Rockingham which was made in one of a hundred other potteries. It is not correct, therefore, to identify an item as "Bennington" and another as "Rockingham." The proper terminology is "Bennington Rockingham," or simply "Rockingham" if the place of manufacture is unknown.

The brown color in American Rockingham is inherent in the glaze itself. This was spattered on by dipping a paddle into a vat of glaze and striking the paddle on the edge of the vat. The spatter was allowed to fall onto the piece of pottery being rotated below. Variations in coloring were achieved by applying the glaze more heavily in some spots, by permitting it to streak, by thinning it or by other intentional or accidental means. It is easy to understand why no two examples of Rockingham are exactly alike in glazing.

Until about 1856 the United States Pottery Company, under Fenton's supervision, used a double-firing process for making its Rockingham ware. A glossy underglaze was applied to the already fired biscuit piece. This glaze was then air-dried before the brown glaze was applied. The use of this underglaze resulted in a finished product of exceptional quality and brilliance. However, from 1856 to 1860 the firm gave up this underglazing of its Rockingham ware in an attempt to economize and during this period produced wares which have little to recommend them. Careful examination of the bottom of a Rockingham piece will usually show whether an underglaze was applied before the brown glaze.

Another popular glaze used on Bennington items was flint enamel, which was really a new process patented in November, 1849, by Christopher Webber Fenton under the name "Fenton's Enamel." This patent was concerned wholly with the method of glazing. Colors under a glaze had been successfully produced as early as 1846 by Bennett & Brothers of Pittsburgh, later of Baltimore. Bennett had applied his color on a biscuit piece of pottery with a brush or sponge, plac-

ing it exactly where he wanted it for decorative purposes, then drying the piece, covering it with glaze and firing it. Fenton, however, gave the biscuit piece a coat of transparent glaze before he applied his new powdered color. Because of the new use of color and the resemblance to an enamel, the type of flint-glaze ware developed by Fenton was called "flint enamel."

Various metallic oxides—cobalt for blue, copper for green, manganese for brown—were finely powdered and then, as he explained in *Letters Patent No. 6907,* dated November 27, 1849, "with a small box perforated with holes, the colors are thrown or sprinkled on through the holes over the surface of the article in quantity to produce deeper or lighter shades, as may be desired, leaving a part of the surface for the body of the articles to show through in spots." When a piece treated in this way was fired, the powdered colors melted and fused with the underglaze, flowing and spreading over the surface of the article. Actually, the position of the piece within the kiln may be determined by the direction in which the melted colors have flowed. When the color was sprinkled lightly the appearance is that of a Rockingham glaze with color added.

Bennington-made flint enamel wares are frequently marked with Fenton's 1849 mark A, with the variations B, C and D found only rarely. Many of the impressed marks on known examples became so filled with glaze that they are almost undecipherable today. A great deal of the flint enamel output was unmarked. The use of the 1849 Fenton mark, with its variations, was not restricted to flint enamel items; it was also used on Rockingham items and, in some instances, Parian porcelain articles. There is no apparent reason for this except possibly carelessness on the part of the workmen, who may have regarded it only as a manufacturer's identification.

Fenton's little-known scroddled ware, sometimes called lava ware or solid agate ware, has frequently been confused with the more easily made marbled ware, which was never made at Bennington and which has surface decoration only. Scroddled ware is composed of different colored clays (usually brown to reddish-brown and gray) mixed with cream-colored clay. The various colored clays were mixed together in such a way that the striations went through the entire piece and are visible both inside and outside; even chips or fragments of scroddled ware items show the variegated layers. The mixed clay was either turned on a wheel or pressed into a mold and the finished piece coated with a clear glaze composed mainly of feldspar and flint and then fired. The variegated clay fused together, rather like a marble cake, with a solid body of different mixed striations.

Scroddled ware was not produced in quantity at Bennington because there was little demand for it and the process was slow and costly. There was some attempt to use a mixture of gray and black and occasionally a pink shade, but very little of this type was produced and examples in such color combinations are quite rare. Items most commonly found in scroddled ware include pitchers, toilet sets and, more rarely, tulip vases, cow creamers, book flasks, toby pitchers and cuspidors. When the items are marked it is usually with the United States Pottery Company's "oval" mark H, although one known book flask does bear the Fenton mark E.

So far, mention has been made of only the Bennington pottery items, which are generally made from the coarser wares. The porcelain articles include some of the finest wares made in America. The difference between pottery and porcelain, both made from clay, shaped and hardened by heat, lies in the degree of opacity. Articles through which light cannot be seen are correctly called pottery or earthenware. But if the article is made of a translucent material, it is called porcelain, whether the article is fine or coarse, glazed or unglazed. The term "china" is synonymous with the term "porcelain."

Parian ware, a hard porcelain resembling marble in texture, translucent, highly vitreous and with a fine granular surface, was introduced in America by Fenton. For a time he was assisted by John Harrison, a modeler from the Copeland works in Stoke-on-Trent, England, where Parian ware had been introduced about 1842. It was first known as "Statuary Ware," as it was expressly designed to imitate Parian marble statues. Fenton made many items in Parian ware in addition to the early figures copied from English designs. Plaster models were used to make molds from which a variety of figures and ornaments were produced.

FIGURE XII. PLASTER MODELS FOR MAKING MOLDS. Pottery workers first carved designs for decorative items in hard plaster. Finished porcelain articles were cast in the molds made from these models. (Compare C with Pls. 241F and 241G.)

The identification of Parian items as Bennington-made is invariably difficult. Unless the design can be documented or is known to be an exclusive Bennington creation, many unmarked Parian pieces cannot be distinguished from similar articles made by Copeland, Alcock, Minton or other English or American manufacturers.

The term "Parian" is applied correctly only when the piece has no exterior glaze or color, so that the resemblance to marble is obvious. If the outside of a piece is glazed, it should

20

be referred to simply as white porcelain. The porcelain finishes range from a high, glossy glaze to a thin, soft smear-glaze.

The most common type of colored porcelain made at Bennington was the blue and white variety, commonly used for pitchers, vases, cologne bottles and trinket boxes. In the best years of the Fenton pottery the distinctive blue coloring was obtained by adding oxide of cobalt to some of the slip. This colored slip was applied directly to the inside of the molds wherever the color was desired and the uncolored clay body then poured into the mold. When the mold was removed the colored slip had become a part of the wall of the article. When it was fired the two materials were fused as one, because except for the difference in color, both were of the same basic composition. If there is a fracture or chip in the blue of a blue and white porcelain article, identification is easy since the blue has an actual thickness in the wall of the piece. From 1858 to 1860, however, this method of applying the color was abandoned as too expensive and time-consuming. Sub-sequently color was painted on the surface of the biscuit piece and the piece refired when the interior glaze was applied.

Blue and white porcelain articles do not always have a pitted blue background, although a few designs were never produced in any other form. The pitted surface, which has a close resemblance to orange peel, was laboriously achieved in the model, with each pinpoint placed separately by hand. This characteristic, however, is only an aid to identification and not positive proof that the piece was made in Bennington. Examples made by T. J. and J. Mayer of England also show a pitted blue background.

Colored porcelain other than blue and white is rare, but examples have been found of several shades of tan and white, pink and white and green and white. There are also examples of articles decorated in various colors which have been painted on a Parian surface and the embellished pieces subsequently fired. These items are rarely found in Bennington-made wares, and caution should be exercised in positively identifying them.

SECTION I: FUNCTIONAL ITEMS

——•——

CHAPTER ONE: PITCHERS

Pitchers were made in almost every type of ware at Bennington. For convenience, they have been divided here into groups which have a resemblance in design, shape or pattern and are also grouped to some degree by material. Some pitchers were part of toilet sets (pitcher and washbowl) and may be found in Chapter Three, "Kitchen and Household Accessories." Toby pitchers are included in Chapter Seven, "Novelty Items," as are miniature pitchers, jugs and vases. Ewers are listed in Chapter Four, "Vases, Ewers, Cologne Bottles and Trinket Boxes."

The earliest Rockingham pitchers made at Bennington during the Norton-Fenton partnership (1845-1847) were the brown-glazed ones impressed with the firm name, town and state. Usually this mark appears in two lines: "Norton & Fenton" on the top line and "Bennington, Vt." or "East Bennington, Vt." on the bottom line. More rare, from a collector's point of view, is the placement of the words in a circle. These early Rockingham pitchers were not spattered but were dipped into a glaze made of red lead, feldspar, flint and clay, with some manganese to supply the brown color.

Many of the pitchers made in Parian porcelain at the Fenton pottery were also made in blue and white porcelain and occasionally in other materials. Many of the Bennington patterns were greatly influenced by, if not directly copied from, English designs. Such designs as the Pond Lily pattern, Love and War and the Good Samaritan are exact copies of their English forerunners. But the Corn Husk motif, which is extremely rare, is one of the few truly original American designs.

Parian pitchers were almost invariably glazed inside. Almost all of the blue and white porcelain pitchers were glazed inside; only a few were also glazed outside. Some of the Parian pitchers were elaborately decorated with clusters of grapes, leaves and tendrils, all applied onto the body of the molded pitchers. Occasionally flowers were applied. No known examples of marked pitchers with applied decoration are known. When Parian pitchers were marked, the mark used was Fenton's Works mark E, the United States Pottery Company "ribbon" mark F, the United States Pottery Company "lozenge" mark G and, extremely rarely, the 1849 mark A.

PLATE 21. WILD ROSE PATTERN PITCHER. 1853-1858. Extremely rare colored example. The roses are glazed reds and pinks, the leaves greens, browns, and yellows, handle brown, marked with U.S.P. "lozenge" mark G, 10¼″ high. This pattern is usually found in Parian or glazed white porcelain. (See also Pls. 90 and 92.)

PLATE 22. EARLY ROCKINGHAM (or DARK-LUSTER) PITCHERS. Made only between 1844-1847. Always impressed on bottom with firm name of "NORTON & FENTON" in two lines. *Top row:* A. Rare size, 7″ high; B. 8¾″ high. *Bottom row:* C. 11″ high; D. 10″ high.

24

PLATE 23. EARLY ROCKINGHAM PITCHERS. Made only between 1844-1847. Always impressed on bottom with firm name of "NORTON & FENTON." *Top row:* A. Rare size, 6½" high. *Bottom row:* B. 8½" high; C. 8⅜" high; A. and B. are marked with extremely rare circle mark.

PLATE 24. FLINT ENAMEL PITCHERS. 1849-1858. All impressed with 1849 mark A. *Top row:* Tulip and Heart pattern, 8 panels with small heart design at top of each rib. A. 10″ high; B. 7¾″ high; C. 6½″ high; D. 5¾″ high. *Bottom row:* Alternate Rib pattern. (For a variant see Pl. 25G.) E. 10½″ high; F. 8½″ high; G. 6¾″ high; H. 6″ high.

PLATE 25. ROCKINGHAM AND FLINT ENAMEL PITCHERS. *Top row:* A. Rockingham, rare shape, 1847-1858, 3¾″ high; B. Diamond pattern, Rockingham, 1847-1858, rare size, 6⅛″ high. (See also Pls. 30A, 30B and 30C.) C. Rockingham, extremely rare shape, 1849-1858, impressed with 1849 mark A, 6⅞″ high; D. Rockingham, 1849-1858, impressed with 1849 mark A, 5¼″ high. (See also Pl. 29B.) *Bottom row:* Flint enamel, uncommon pattern with mask lip, 1849-1858, impressed with 1849 mark A, 9″ high; F. Hunting scene, 8″ high. (See also Pls. 26C, 26D and 26E.) ; G. Flint enamel, rare Swirled Alternate Rib pattern, 1849-1858, impressed with 1849 mark A, 10″ high.

26

PLATE 26. FLINT ENAMEL AND ROCKINGHAM PITCHERS. *Top row:* A. Flint enamel, 1849-1858. Brilliantly colored with blues, greens and browns, 9″ high; B. Flint enamel, 1849-1858, Scalloped Rib body, uncommon design, marked with only known example of 1849 mark B, 9″ high. *Bottom row:* Three Rockingham Hunting Scene pattern pitchers, 1847-1858. C. 9″ high; D. 8½″ high; E. 7″ high.

PLATE 27. ROCKINGHAM AND FLINT ENAMEL PITCHERS. A. Rockingham, 1847-1858, 6″ high; B. Rockingham, extremely rare size and design mask lip pitcher, 1847-1858, 4½″ high; C. Flint enamel creamer, 1849-1858, 6⅜″ high. (Same shape as Pl. 135A, except has raised band around neck. See also Pl. 167B.)

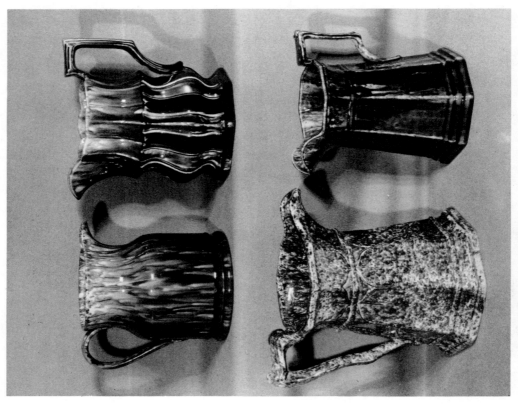

PLATE 29. FLINT ENAMEL AND ROCKINGHAM PITCHERS. *Top row:* Flint enamel, 1849-1858, 9″ high; B. Rockingham, 1847-1858, 10½″ high. (See also Pl. 25D.) *Bottom row:* C. Gothic design, Rockingham, 1847 (at least), 11¼″ high; D. Flint enamel, 9¾″ high.

PLATE 28. BARREL-SHAPED PITCHERS. *Top row:* A. Flint enamel, 1849-1858, 6″ high. *Bottom row:* B. Rockingham, 1847-1858, 5⅛″ high; C. Rockingham, 1847-1858, 5⅛″ high.

28

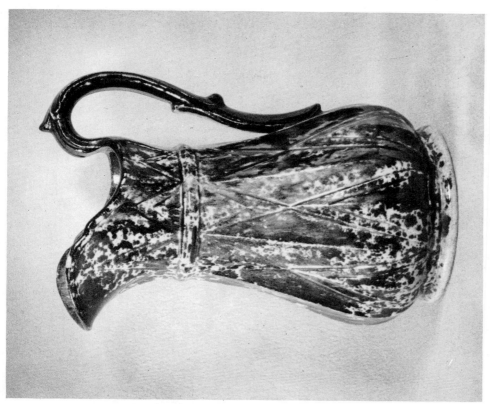

PLATE 31. DIAMOND PATTERN ROCKINGHAM PITCHER. 1853-1858, the only known example in this glaze (it is usually found in flint enamel or scroddled ware), part of a washbowl set, 11⅛" high. (See also Pl. 39D.)

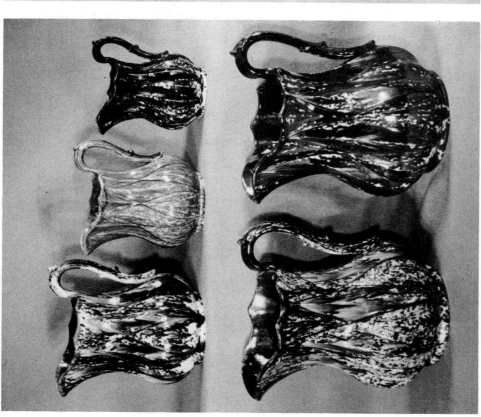

PLATE 30. DIAMOND PATTERN FLINT ENAMEL PITCHERS. 1849-1858. Rare pattern. *Top row:* A. Dark browns and greens, 1849 mark A, 8¾" high: B. Light brown and yellow, 1849 mark A, 7½" high; C. Dark browns and orange, 6½" high. *Bottom row:* D. Extremely rare beaded frame around diamond, dark browns and bright green on cream background, 1849 mark A, 11" high; E. Dark browns and orange, 11¼" high.

29

PLATE 32. HOUND-HANDLED PITCHER. These were always in Rockingham and were made in four sizes: 6-qt., 4-qt., 3-qt., and 2-qt. Three points of identification must always be present to distinguish Bennington origin: (1) The hound's long duck-billed nose rests in paws, but with the neck arched so one's little finger may fit underneath. (2) The collar is made of links rather than a band or strap. (3) The underside of hound is sharp-edged, not flattened or rounded. No marked example has ever been found. 1852-1867 (at least). 8¾" high. (CAUTION, compare with Pls. 35, 36 and 37.)

PLATE 33. HOUND-HANDLED PITCHERS. This illustration compares the largest size, 6-qt., with the smallest, 2-qt. A. 6-qt. size, 11¼″ high; B. 2-qt. size, 8¾″ high. (CAUTION, compare with Pls. 35, 36 and 37.)

PLATE 34. HOUND-HANDLED PITCHERS. *Top row:* A. Extremely rare example, with branch handle on body of hound pitcher, 11″ high; B. 9½″ high. *Bottom row:* C. 8¾″ high; D. 9¾″ high; E. 9″ high. This illustration shows the variety in richness of the Rockingham glaze. (CAUTION, compare with Pls. 35, 36 and 37.)

PLATE 35. COMPARISON PIECES, NOTE CAREFULLY. A. Made by Ballard Bros., Burlington, Vt., 9″ high; B. Made by Harker, Taylor Co., East Liverpool, Ohio, 8″ high. Both of these pieces were made about 1850.

PLATE 36. Comparison Pieces, Note Carefully. Two examples of 4-quart size hound-handled pitchers. A. Made in Bennington, 11¼″ high. Compare with B, made by and impressed on bottom, "Vance Faience Pottery Co." in Tiltonville, Ohio, from Bennington molds, 11¼″ high. The Vance glazes are not Rockingham, but varieties of orange shading to brown, as in this specimen, also a blue and white Delft-like high glaze and a matte green glaze.

PLATE 37. Comparison Pieces, Note Carefully. Three examples of 2-quart hound-handled pitchers. A. Made by Nichols & Alford, Burlington, Vt., 8¼″ high, note difference in hound; B. Bennington-made, 9″ high; C. Made by J. B. Caire & Co., Po'keepsie, N. Y., 9⅝″ high.

PLATE 38. Scroddled Ware Pitchers. 1853-1858, marked with U.S.P. "oval" mark H. A. Shades of brown streaked through cream background, 8¼″ high; B. Red- dish-brown streaks on gray background, part of a wash- bowl set, 12″ high. All items in scroddled ware are extremely rare.

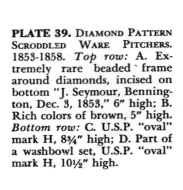

PLATE 39. Diamond Pattern Scroddled Ware Pitchers. 1853-1858. *Top row:* A. Ex- tremely rare beaded frame around diamonds, incised on bottom "J. Seymour, Benning- ton, Dec. 3, 1853," 6″ high; B. Rich colors of brown, 5″ high. *Bottom row:* C. U.S.P. "oval" mark H, 8¾″ high; D. Part of a washbowl set, U.S.P. "oval" mark H, 10½″ high.

34

PLATE 41. GRANITEWARE PITCHER. Only known example of this shape design. Flowers executed in same manner as Pl. 44A. Name of Bennington resident in gold, made at Fenton's Pottery c. 1850, 8¾″ high.

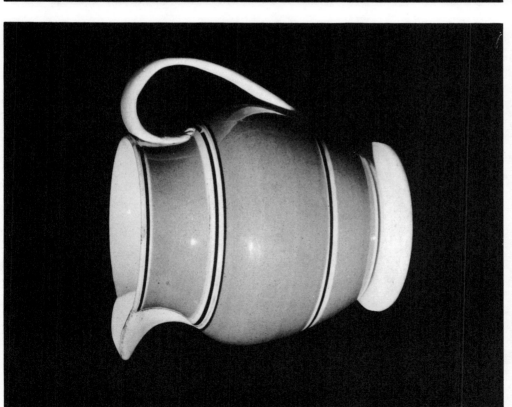

PLATE 40. GRANITEWARE BANDED PITCHER. 1853-1858. Difficult to identify positively without personal history or documentation. Top and bottom bands gray-green, center band gray-blue, stripes black, 7⅛″ high.

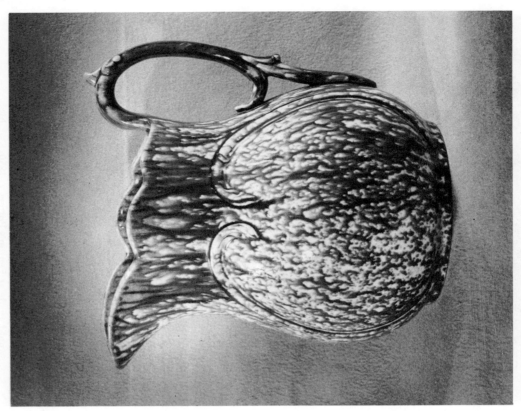

PLATE 43. "SWEETHEART" or "PRESENTATION" PITCHER. Made in Rockingham glaze, only known example, 1850-1858, 9½" high. This design was usually made in graniteware, decorated in gold and blue. (See also Pl. 48.)

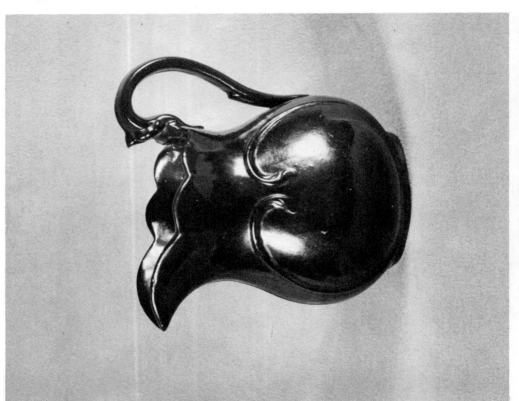

PLATE 42. "SWEETHEART" or "PRESENTATION" PITCHER. 1850-1858. Made of red clay and dipped in solid dark brown slip-like glaze, 7½" high. This is the only known example bearing the inscription incised on the bottom "Hoosic Red Clay."

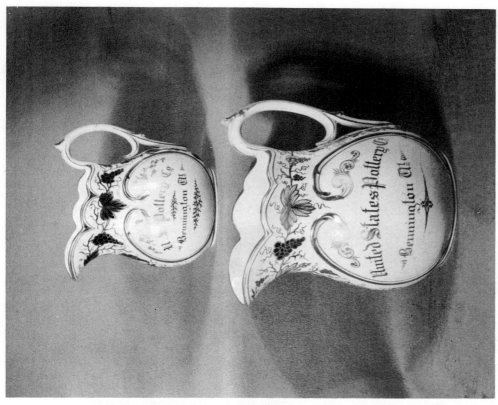

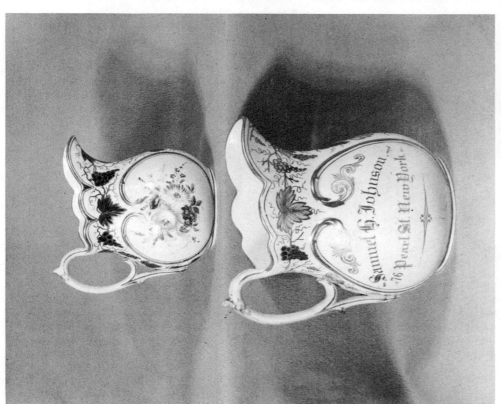

PLATES 44 and 44A. "SWEETHEART" or "PRESENTA-
TION" PITCHERS. Made in graniteware. 1853-1858. Reverse and obverse. Decorated in gold and colors, flowers
in shades of rose and pink, leaves green, grapes blue.
Mr. Johnson was Vice President of United States Pottery Co. A. Smaller pitcher, 7½" high; B. Larger pitcher,
9½" high. (CAUTION, compare with Pl. 49C.)

PLATE 45. "Sweetheart" or "Presentation" Pitcher. Graniteware, 1850-1858, extremely rare use of rose-pink background, hunting dog in gold. Leaves edged in green and gold, owner's name on obverse, 6½" high. (Caution, compare with Pl. 49C.)

PLATE 46. "Sweetheart" or "Presentation" Pitcher and Matching Cup. Made in graniteware for Stark Lodge, IOOF, in Bennington, 1850-1858, extremely rare rose-pink background color with lodge symbols in gold. Cup 4¼" high; Pitcher, 9¾" high. (Caution, compare with Pl. 49C.)

PLATE 47. "Sweetheart" or "Presentation" Pitchers. Graniteware, 1850-1858. *Top row:* A. Extremely rare use of magenta background color with green leaves, 9¾" high. Note lack of bridge in handle. *Bottom row:* B. Reverse of pitcher, obverse bearing owner's name in gold. Flowers in gold, leaves and grapes in blue, 9¼" high; C. Extremely rare use of dark red background color with blue leaf-shaped decorations, 9⅜" high. Note lack of bridge in handle. (Caution, compare with Pl. 49C.)

38

PLATE 48. "Sweetheart" or "Presentation" Pitchers. Graniteware, all known sizes. 1850-1858. There are no known marked examples of this type of pitcher. *Top row:* A. 4⅜" high; B. 4⅜" high; C. 4½" high; D. 4⅞" high (This type is extremely difficult to identify positively without personal history or documentation); E. 6½" high. *Bottom row:* F. Only known example with yellow background color, 9½" high; G. 8½" high; H. 8¼" high; I. 7½" high. (CAUTION, compare with Pl. 49C.)

PLATE 49. COMPARISON PIECES, NOTE CAREFULLY. Graniteware "presentation" pitchers. A. Braced handle, made at Bennington, 9¾" high; B. Not braced handle, leaf at end, made at Bennington, 9½" high. Compare with C, not braced handle, leaf at end, identical to B, made by Houghwout & Co. Pottery at Greenpoint, Brooklyn. When this pattern pitcher does not have typical decoration (as in Pls. 45, 46, 47, 48), it is impossible to attribute it to Bennington without history or documentation.

PLATE 50. Cascade Pattern Pitcher. Fine example in an uncommon, highly glazed white porcelain. One of Fenton's few original designs, 1847-1848, marked with Fenton's Works mark E, 9¼" high.

PLATE 51. Cascade Pattern Pitchers. A. The even brown color here is probably a stain. Glazed white porcelain, 1853-1858, U.S.P. "lozenge" mark G, 10½" high; B. Parian, glazed inside, 8¼" high.

PLATE 52. CHARTER OAK PATTERN PITCHER. Blue and white porcelain, 1852-1858, U.S.P. "ribbon" mark F, 9½" high.

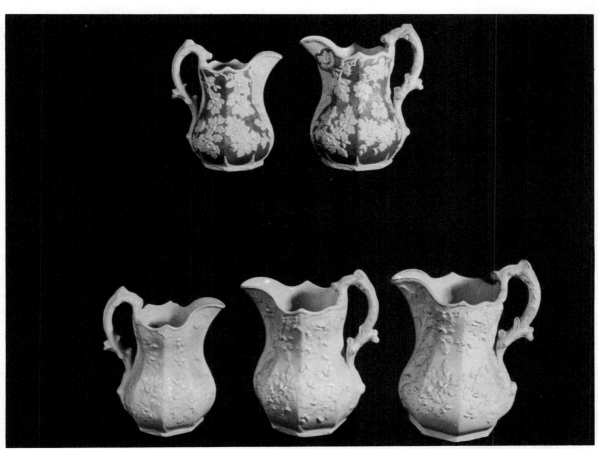

PLATE 53. CHARTER OAK PATTERN PITCHERS. All five pitchers are marked with U.S.P. "ribbon" mark F, 1852-1858. *Top row:* A. Blue and white porcelain, 8" high; B. Blue and white porcelain, 9¼" high. *Bottom row:* C. Graniteware, uncommon material and size, 7½" high; D. Graniteware, uncommon material, 9¾" high; E. Parian, 10½" high.

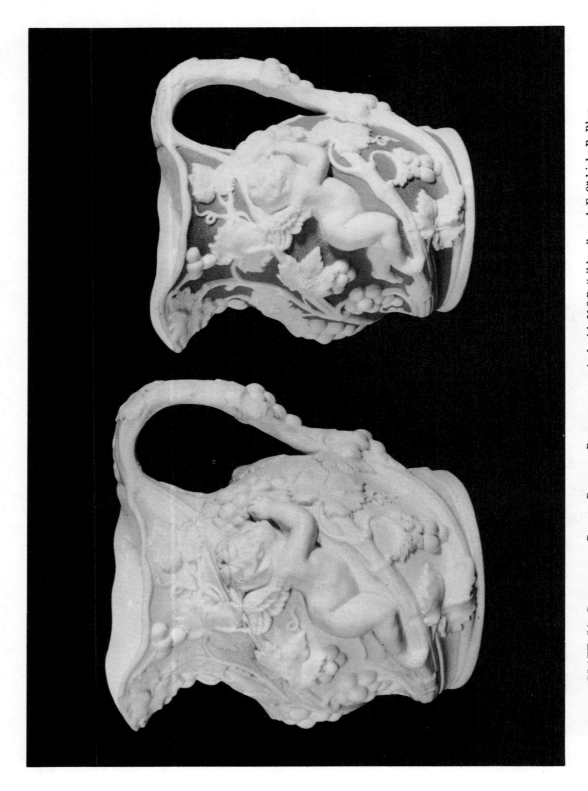

PLATE 54. CHERUB AND GRAPES PATTERN PITCHERS. Extremely rare pattern, a duplicate of pattern made by Wedgwood in England. A. Parian, marked with U.S.P. "ribbon" mark F, 9″ high; B. Blue and white porcelain, 7⅞″ high. It is supposed that both sizes were made in both materials.

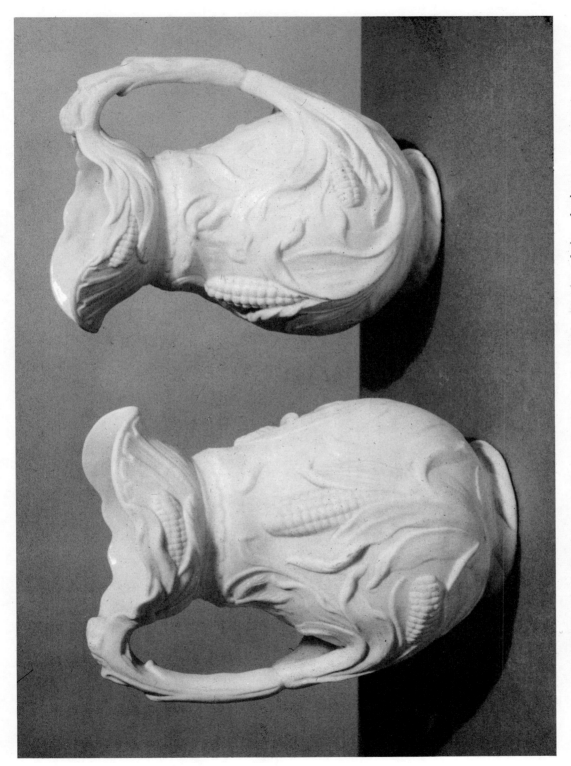

PLATE 55. CORN HUSK PATTERN PARIAN PITCHERS. 1852-1858. Extremely rare pattern, marked with U.S.P. "ribbon" mark F, 9⅝" high. This pattern is one of the few purely American designs, having no counterpart in English wares.

PLATE 56. Cupid and Psyche Pattern Pitcher. Only known example in Rockingham, 1850-1858, 6″ high. (See also Pls. 105H and 110.)

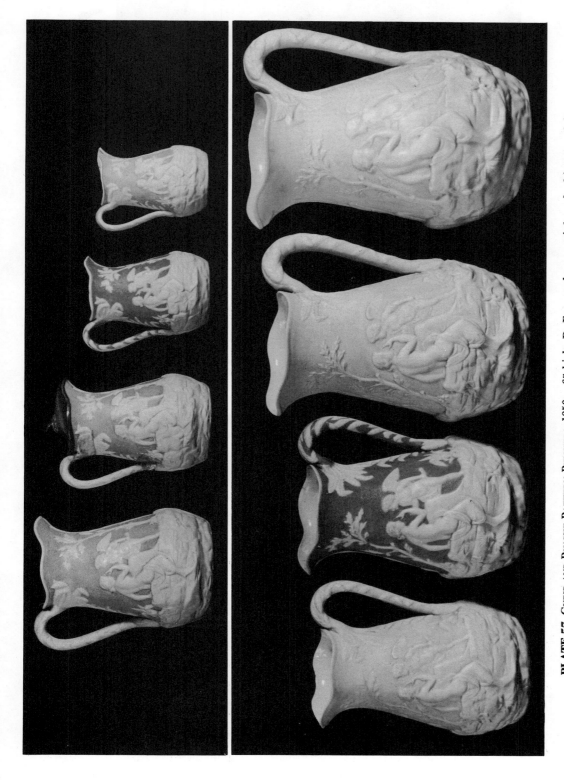

PLATE 57. CUPID AND PSYCHE PATTERN PITCHERS. 1850-1858. *Top row:* A. Extremely rare pink and white porcelain, 8¼" high; B. Extremely rare pink and white porcelain, 7" high; C. Rare blue and white porcelain, 6" high; D. Extremely rare pink and white porcelain, 5¼" high. *Bottom row:* E. Parian, 8¼" high; F. Rare blue and white porcelain, 9" high; G. Parian, 10" high; H. Parian, 11" high. (See also Pls. 56 and 110.)

45

PLATE 58. DAFFODIL PATTERN PARIAN PITCHERS. 1847-1858. Extremely rare pattern. A. Only known example this size, 11" high (See also Pl. 105.); B. 4½" high.

PLATE 59. GEOMETRIC ARABESQUE PATTERN PITCHER. Mask lip. 1850-1858. Extremely rare pattern in either material. A. Graniteware, 7" high; B. Highly glazed blue and white porcelain, extremely rare treatment, 6¾" high. (See also Pl. 108A.)

PLATE 60. THE GOOD SAMARITAN PATTERN PITCHER. 1847-1848. Smear-glazed porcelain, rare design, marked with Fenton's Works mark A, 5″ high. Obverse and reverse of this pattern, frequently erroneously called "Gypsy" design. When unmarked, it is very difficult to distinguish this pattern from a similar one made by Jones and Walley in England. (CAUTION, compare with Pls. 61A and 61B.)

PLATE 61. COMPARISON PIECES, NOTE CAREFULLY. A. The Good Samaritan pattern Parian pitcher, sometimes called erroneously the Gypsy pattern, made in Bennington by C. W. Fenton, 1847-1858, 5″ high. (See also Pl. 60.) Compare with B, made by and marked Jones & Walley, Cobridge, England, 4⅞″ high. This mark is similar to Fenton's Works mark A.

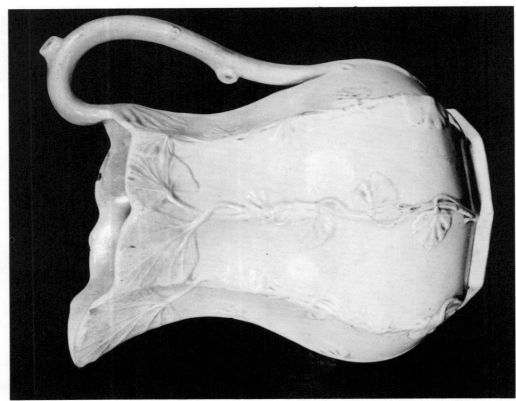

PLATE 63. Ivy Vine Pattern Pitcher. Graniteware, 1850-1858, extremely rare pattern, incised on bottom with bench mark "No. 1Z," 9½" high. (See also Pls. 62 and 204B.)

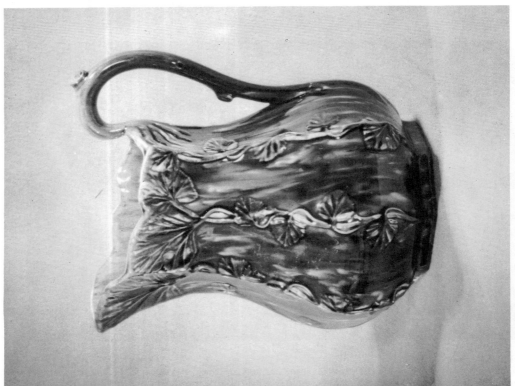

PLATE 62. Ivy Vine Pattern Pitcher. Flint enamel, 1849-1858, extremely rare pattern, marked with 1849 mark A, 10" high. This Ivy Vine pattern was also used on picture frames. (See also Pl. 204B.)

48

PLATE 64. LILY PAD PATTERN PITCHERS. Blue and white porcelain. 1850-1858. This leaf design was a popular motif, appearing in many variants. (See also Pls. 103C, 228, 232, 251, 276G, 290.) A. 10" high; B. 11" high; C. 10" high.

PLATE 65. LOVE AND WAR PATTERN PARIAN PITCHER. 1847-1848. Obverse and reverse of one of the loveliest pitchers made in Parian. Extremely rare design, marked with Fenton's Works mark E, 7″ high. Direct copy of similar pitcher made by Samuel Alcock in England. (CAUTION, compare with Pls. 66A and 66B.)

PLATE 66. COMPARISON PIECES, NOTE CAREFULLY. A. Parian Love and War pitcher, marked with Fenton's Works mark E, 7″ high. (See also Pl. 65.) Compare with B, made by and marked Sam'l Alcock, England. Raised design is in Alcock purple. Both of these pitchers are extremely rare articles from either pottery.

PLATE 67. PARIAN PORCELAIN PITCHER. Only known example of this design, this pitcher was illustrated in *Old China*, a magazine for collectors published in 1901. Glazed inside, c. 1850, 8½" high.

PLATE 68. PANELED GRAPEVINE PITCHERS. Rare design, regardless of material used. A. Blue and white porcelain, 1850-1858, 8¼" high; B. Graniteware, blue-gray color, 1850-1858, 8⅝" high.

PLATE 69. PANELED GRAPEVINE PITCHERS. A. Rockingham, 1852-1858, 7¾" high; B. Graniteware, 1852-1858, 8⅜" high. Pitchers in this design, regardless of size or materials used, are rare.

PLATE 70. TWO RARE-PATTERNED PITCHERS. A. Paneled Acanthus Leaf pattern, flint enamel, 1849-1858, 11¾" high; B. Paneled Grapevine pattern, 1852-1858, 11¼" high. (See also Pls. 68A, 68B and 69.)

PLATE 71. PANELED VINE AND FLOWER PATTERN PITCHERS. 1847-1848. A. Parian creamer, has matching sugar bowl, 5″ high (See also Pl. 113) ; B. Smear-glazed outside, highly glazed inside, Fenton's Works mark E, 8″ high; C. Smear-glazed outside, U.S.P. "lozenge" mark G, rare size, 9¾″ high.

PLATE 72. PAUL AND VIRGINIA PATTERN PITCHER. Extremely rare example in this solid brown slip-like glaze, 1852-1858, U.S.P. "ribbon" mark F, 9¾" high.

PLATE 73. PAUL AND VIRGINIA PATTERN PITCHER. Only known example of this pattern in graniteware, very coarse and heavy, 1847-1858, 7½″ high.

PLATE 74. Comparison Pieces, Note Carefully. Paul and Virginia pattern. Blue and white porcelain pitchers. *Top row:* A. Made by T. J. and J. Mayer, England, 9¾″ high. The English pattern is slimmer, with a more pronounced bulge at base. Compare with B, marked with U.S.P. "ribbon" mark F, 9½″ high. The Bennington-made pattern has a more snub-nosed lip, and greater curve to handle. *Bottom row:* C. T. J. and J. Mayer, England, 11¼″ high. In the English pattern the figures of Paul and Virginia are larger in relation to the foliage. Compare with D, marked with U.S.P. "ribbon" mark F, 11″ high. The blue is consistently darker in the Bennington-made pieces. (See also Pls. 72, 73, 76 and 77A.)

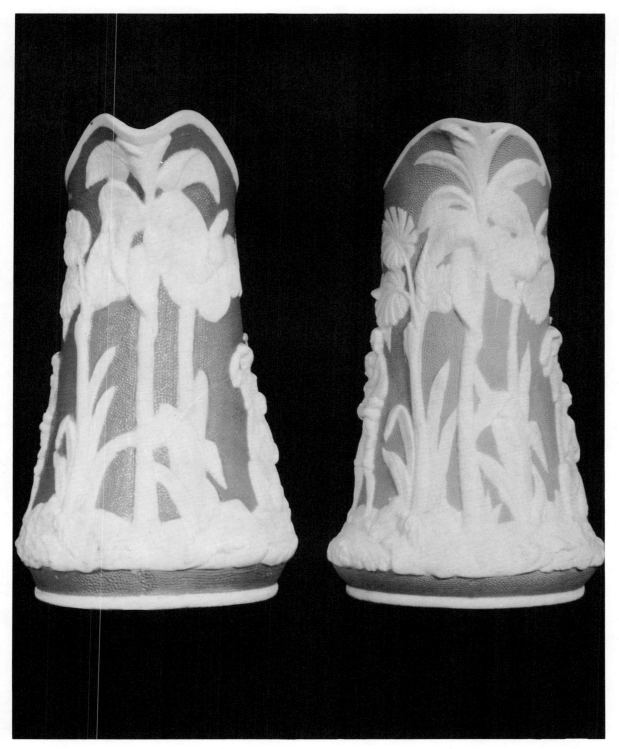

PLATE 75. COMPARISON PIECES, NOTE CAREFULLY. A. Bennington-made. Note relationship of leaves, and curve of pitcher lip. Important easy clue is that in the Bennington-made design, under side of lip has solid leaves, no blue color, while English example always has two small spots of color showing between leaves. Compare with B, made by T. J. and J. Mayer. Note two spots of color between leaves under lip, also the relationship of foliage of figures.

PLATE 76. PAUL AND VIRGINIA PATTERN PITCHERS. Blue and white porcelain, 1852-1858, marked with U.S.P. "ribbon" mark F. A. 11″ high; B. 10½″ high; C. 9½″ high. (CAUTION, compare with Pls. 74 and 75.)

PLATE 77. Two Gray-Green Porcelain Pitchers. Only known examples with this color background, 1852-1858, U.S.P. "ribbon" mark F. A. Paul and Virginia pattern, note brace in handle 9″ high; B. Pond Lily pattern, 7¾″ high. (Caution, compare with Pls. 74, 75 and 79.)

PLATE 78. POND LILY PATTERN PITCHER. Only known
example in red-brown slip-like glaze, 1849-1858, 1849
mark A on bottom, 10″ high.

PLATE 79. COMPARISON PIECE, NOTE CAREFULLY.
Pond Lily Parian pitcher. Made by and marked Copeland, with registry date, June 1851, 6¼" high (Compare
this with Pls. 77B, 78, 80, 81 and 82.)

PLATE 80. Pond Lily Pattern Pitchers. 1852-1858, U.S.P. "ribbon" mark F. A. Parian, 8½″ high; B. Blue and white porcelain, 8½″ high; C. Graniteware, extremely rare, 8½″ high. (Caution, see also Pl. 79.)

PLATE 81. Pond Lily Pattern Pitchers. Parian porcelain, 1850-1858. A. 4¼" high; B. 7" high; C. 8½" high; D. 9¾" high. C and D marked with U.S.P. "ribbon" mark F. (Caution, compare with Pl. 79.)

PLATE 82. POND LILY PATTERN PITCHER. Only known example in Rockingham, 1852-1858, U.S.P. "ribbon" mark F, 10¼" high.

PLATE 83. Pond Lily and Acanthus Leaf Pattern
Pitcher. Only known example, Parian porcelain, 1852-
1858, U.S.P. "ribbon" mark F, 10⅝" high.

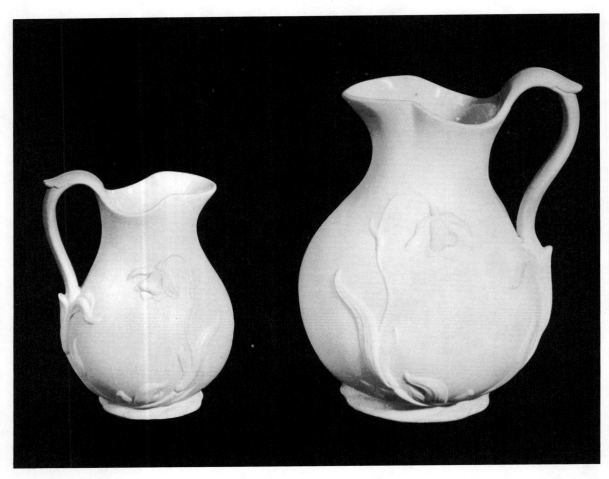

PLATE 84. SNOWDROP PATTERN PARIAN PITCHERS. 1848. Extremely rare design, marked with Fenton's Works mark E. This is one of the rarest designs produced at Bennington, copied from a design by Henry Fitz-Cook of England. A. 6″ high; B. 8½″ high. (CAUTION, compare with Pls. 85A and 85B.)

PLATE 85. COMPARISON PIECES, NOTE CAREFULLY. Extremely rare Snowdrop design. A. Parian, marked with Fenton's Works mark E, 8¾" high (See also Pl. 84.) When this pattern is unmarked, compare closely with B for slight differences in thickness of neck and curve of handle. B. Light blue-gray smear glaze, 9¼" high. English design by Henry Fitz-Cook, registered in January, 1848. Color is an easy identification, but when found in Parian, it is almost necessary to compare it with a Bennington-made specimen to notice slight differences of form and shape.

PLATE 86. TULIP AND SUNFLOWER PATTERN PITCHER. Only known example in graniteware, plain lip, palm tree, 1852-1858, U.S.P. "ribbon" mark F, 8½" high. (CAUTION, compare with Pls. 91A and 91B.)

68

PLATE 87. TULIP AND SUNFLOWER PATTERN PITCHER. Only known example of this pattern in blue and white porcelain, 1852-1858, U.S.P. "ribbon" mark F, 8½" high. (CAUTION, compare with Pls. 91A and 91B.)

PLATE 88. Tulip and Sunflower Pattern Pitchers. All top row are Parian, 1852-1858, with mask up, scallop band. *Top row:* A. 5⅜" high; B. 5¾" high; C. 7½" high; D. 9½" high. *Bottom row:* E. Plain lip, palm tree, Parian, 1853-1858, U.S.P. "ribbon mark" F, 8½" high; F. Plain lip, Gothic scallop band, 1847-1853, Fenton's Works mark E, 8½" high; G. Glazed porcelain, 1853-1858, U.S.P. "ribbon" mark F, 8⅞" high. (Caution, compare with Pls. 91A and 91B.)

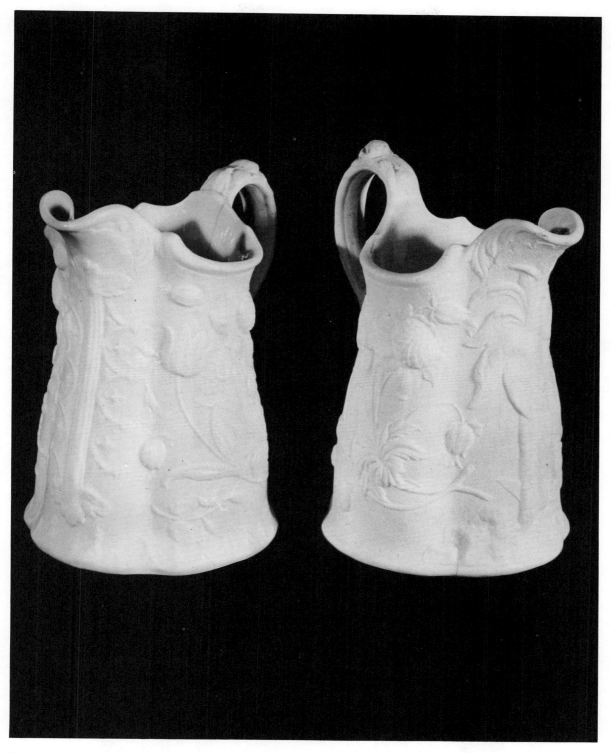

PLATE 89. TULIP AND SUNFLOWER PATTERN PITCHERS. Both are Parian, 1857-1858, without mask under lip. A. Scalloped band under lip and around bottom, marked with U.S.P. "lozenge" mark G, 8¼" high; B. Palm tree under lip, plain bottom, marked with U.S.P. "ribbon" mark F, 8" high.

PLATE 90. Tulip and Sun-flower Pattern and Wild Rose Pattern Pitchers. Top row shows the three variations of the design under lip of pitcher. *Top row:* A. Palm tree, without inverted Gothic scallops around base, Parian, 1852-1858, U.S.P. "ribbon" mark F, 8½" high; B. Mask under lip with Gothic scallop band, Parian, 1853-1858, 7⅝" high; C. Gothic scallop band, Parian, 1853-1858, U.S.P. "loz-enge" mark G, 8½" high. *Bottom row:* D. Wild Rose pattern in cream buff porcelain bisque, 1853-1858, 10½" high; E. Same as Pl. 21. (Caution, compare A, B and C with Pls. 91A and 91B.)

PLATE 91. Comparison Pieces, Note Carefully. A. Tulip and Sunflower pattern, Bennington-made, marked with U.S.P. "ribbon" mark F, 8¾" high. Compare with B, tan and white porcelain, same design, made by and marked "L. W. Clark Co., 1873," 7⅝" high. This pattern was also made in Portugal in a gold and polychrome example.

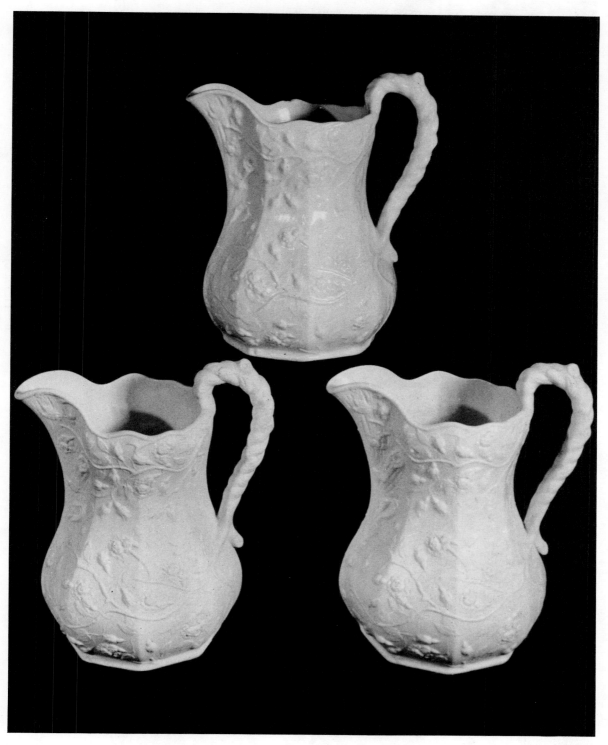

PLATE 92. WILD ROSE PATTERN PITCHERS. 1853-1858. *Top row:* Graniteware, highly glazed, 10″ high. *Bottom row:* B. Parian, glazed inside, 10″ high; C. Smear-glazed white porcelain, glazed inside, 10″ high; U.S.P. "lozenge" mark G. (See also Pl. 21.)

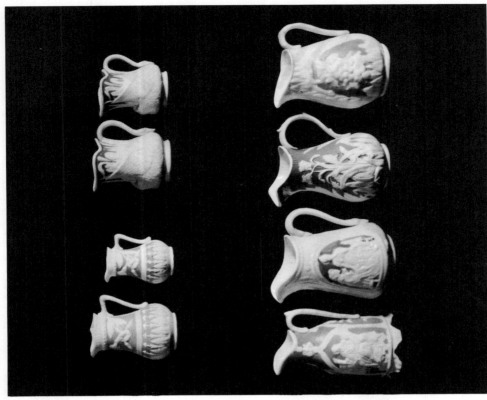

PLATE 94. BLUE AND WHITE PORCELAIN PITCHERS.
1850-1858. *Top row:* A. 4" high; B. 3" high; C. Swan
neck handle, 3¾" high. (See also Pl. 106H.) D. Swan
neck handle, 3" high. (See also Pl. 106H.) *Bottom row:*
E. Apostle pattern, extremely rare, 5⅛" high; F. Spinning Wheel pattern, 5" high. (See also Pls. 102B, 102C,
104C and 104D.); G. 5" high; H. 4¾" high. (See
also Pl. 102A.)

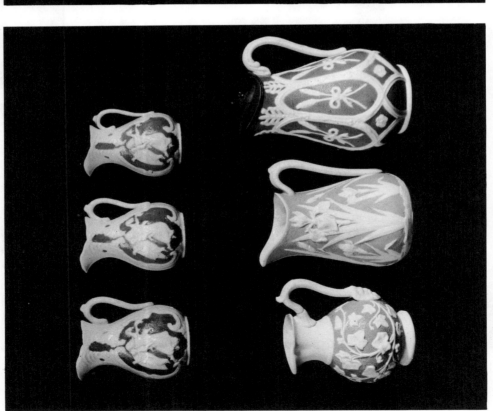

PLATE 93. BLUE AND WHITE PORCELAIN PITCHERS.
1850-1858. *Top row:* Day and Night pattern, highly-
glazed porcelain. A. 5½" high; B. 5" high; C. 4½" high.
(See also Pl. 406A.) *Bottom row:* D. Ivy pattern, mask-
end handle, 6" high; E. Iris pattern, 6½" high; F.
Wheat in panel, 7" high. (See also Pl. 95.)

74

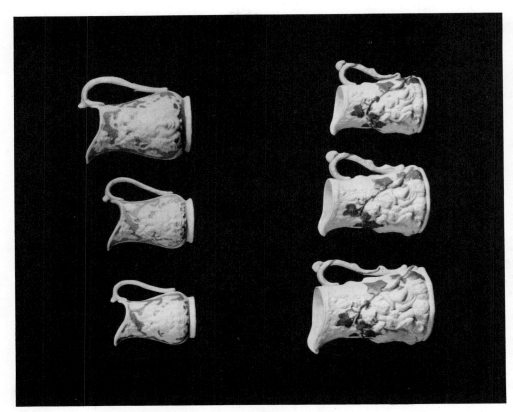

PLATE 96. BLUE AND WHITE PORCELAIN PITCHERS. 1850-1858. *Top row:* Mask design. A. 3½" high; B. 3¾" high; C. 4½" high. *Bottom row:* Babes in the Woods pattern. D. 4¾" high; E. 4¼" high; F. 3¾" high. (See also Pl. 96D.)

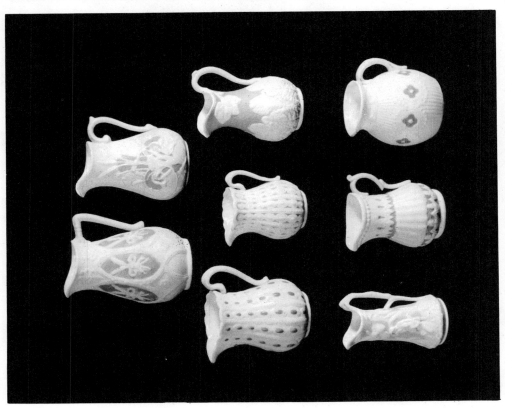

PLATE 95. BLUE AND WHITE PORCELAIN PITCHERS. 1850-1858. *Top row:* A. 5¼" high (See also Pl. 93F.); B. 4½" high. *Center row:* C. 4¼" high (See also Pl. 106C.); D. 3¼" high (See also Pl. 106C.); E. 4¼" high. *Bottom row:* F. Paul and Virginia, extremely rare size, 3¾" high (CAUTION, compare with Pls. 74 and 75.); G. 3½" high (See also Pls. 106D and 106E); H. 3¼" high.

PLATE 97. PALM TREE PATTERN SYRUP PITCHERS. Rare brown and white porcelain, 1852-1858, marked with U.S.P. "ribbon" mark F. A. Light brown with uneven high glaze in green inside, extremely rare coloring, 7¼" high; B. Spoiled in the firing, the brown glaze has a burned metallic cast, 7¼" high; C. Exceptionally fine light brown color, white glaze inside, 7¼" high.

PLATE 98. PALM TREE PATTERN PITCHER. Only known example in dark chocolate brown porcelain, highly glazed inside and out, 1853-1858, U.S.P. "lozenge" mark G, 6¾" high.

PLATE 99. BIRD AND NEST PATTERN SYRUP PITCHERS. Parian, 1853-1858, made for pewter covers. A. Marked with U.S.P. "lozenge" mark G, 7⅜" high; B. 6½" high. (See also Pl. 103D.)

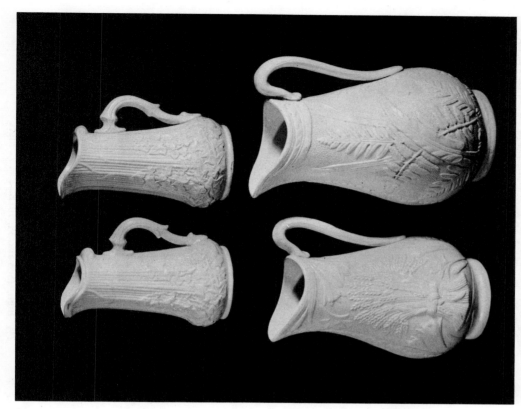

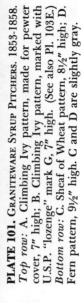

PLATE 101. GRANITEWARE SYRUP PITCHERS. 1853-1858. *Top row*: A. Climbing Ivy pattern, made for pewter cover, 7" high; B. Climbing Ivy pattern, marked with U.S.P. "lozenge" mark G, 7" high. (See also Pl. 103E.) *Bottom row*: C. Sheaf of Wheat pattern, 8½" high; D. Fern pattern, 9½" high. C and D are slightly gray.

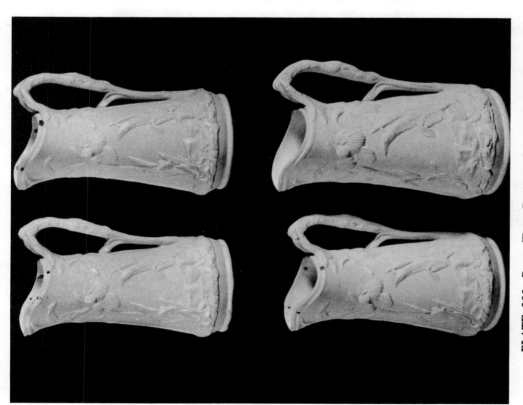

PLATE 100. PALM TREE PATTERN SYRUP PITCHERS. Similar to "Paul and Virginia" pattern (Pls. 72, 73 and 76) but without the figures in relief. 1853-1858. *Top row*: A. Highly-glazed porcelain, U.S.P. "ribbon" mark F, 7⅛" high; B. Smear-glazed porcelain, U.S.P. "lozenge" mark G, 7¼" high. *Bottom row*: C. Parian, U.S.P. "lozenge" mark G, 7⅛" high; D. Parian, U.S.P. "lozenge" mark G, 7½" high.

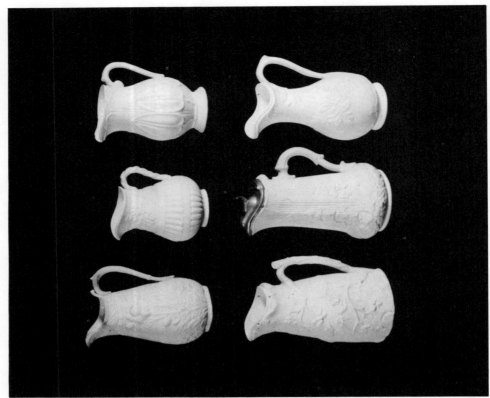

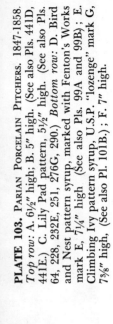

PLATE 103. PARIAN PORCELAIN PITCHERS. 1847-1858. *Top row:* A. 6½" high; B. 5" high. (See also Pls. 441D, 441E.) C. Lily Pad pattern, 5½" high. (See also Pls. 64, 228, 232E, 251, 276G, 290.) *Bottom row:* D. Bird and Nest pattern syrup, marked with Fenton's Works mark E, 7¼" high (See also Pls. 99A and 99B).; E. Climbing Ivy pattern syrup, U.S.P. "lozenge" mark G, 7⅞" high, (See also Pl. 101B.) ; F. 7" high.

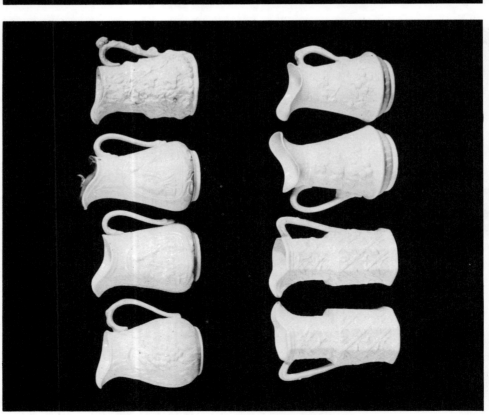

PLATE 102. PARIAN PORCELAIN PITCHERS. 1847-1858. *Top row:* A. 5" high. (See also Pl. 94H.) B. Spinning Wheel pattern, 5" high. (See also Pls. 94F, 104C and 104D.) C. Spinning Wheel pattern, 5⅝" high; D. 4¾" high. (See also Pls. 96D, 96E and 96F.) *Bottom row:* E. and F. 5¾" high; G. 5½" high; H. 5⅛" high.

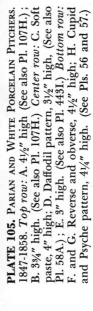

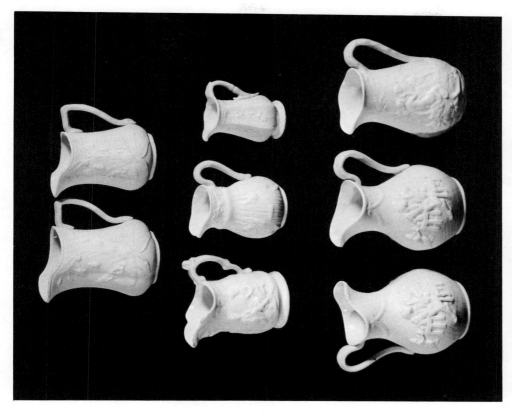

PLATE 105. PARIAN AND WHITE PORCELAIN PITCHERS. 1847-1858. *Top row:* A. 4½" high (See also Pl. 107H.); B. 3¾" high. (See also Pl. 107H.) *Center row:* C. Soft paste, 4" high; D. Daffodil pattern, 3½" high, (See also Pl. 58A.); E. 3" high. (See also Pl. 443I.) *Bottom row:* F. and G. Reverse and obverse, 4½" high; H. Cupid and Psyche pattern, 4¼" high. (See Pls. 56 and 57.)

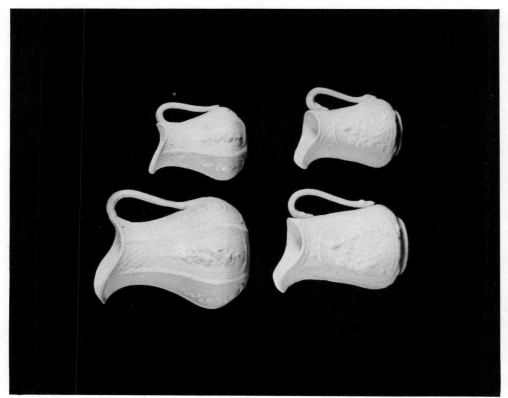

PLATE 104. PARIAN AND WHITE PORCELAIN PITCHERS. 1847-1858. *Top row:* A. 6¼" high; B. 4" high. *Bottom row:* C. Highly glazed, inside and out, 5¼" high (See also Pls. 102B and 102C.); D. Smear-glazed, 4⅛" high, (See also Pls. 102B and 102C.)

79

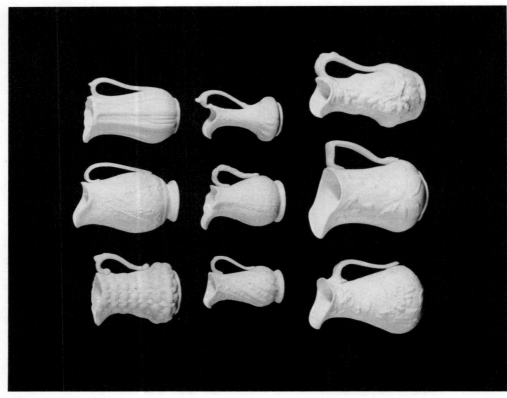

PLATE 107. PARIAN PORCELAIN PITCHERS. 1847-1858.
Top row: A. 3½" high; B. 4½" high; C. 4¼" high.
Center row: D. 3¾" high; E. 3⅝" high; F. 3¾" high.
Bottom row: G. 4½" high; H. 4⅝" high (See also Pls. 105A and 105B.); I. 4½" high.

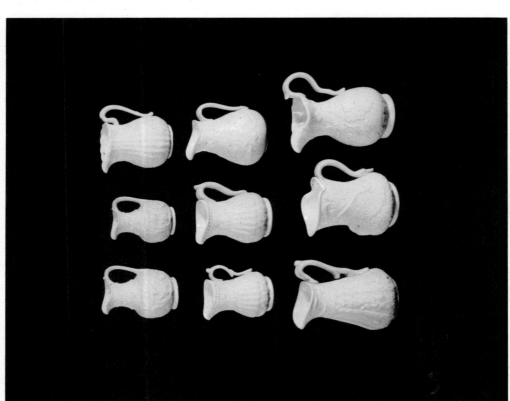

PLATE 106. PARIAN PORCELAIN PITCHERS. 1847-1858.
Top row: A. 4" high; B. 3½" high; C. 3¾" high (See also Pls. 95C and 95D.) *Center row:* D. 3½" high (See also Pl. 95G.); E. 3¾" high (See also Pl. 95G.); F. 4" high. *Bottom row:* G. 4¾" high; H. 4⅛" high (See also Pls. 94C and 94D.); I. 5¼" high.

80

PLATE 108. PARIAN AND WHITE PORCELAIN PITCHERS. 1847-1858. *Top row:* A. Geometric Arabesque pattern, white porcelain, extremely rare pattern, 4¾" high (See also Pls. 59A and 59B.) ; B. 5" high; C. 4½" high. *Center row:* D. 3¾" high; E. Also made in blue and white porcelain, 4" high; F. 4¼" high. *Bottom row:* G. 5¼" high; H. and I. Extremely rare pattern, 1852-1858, marked with U.S.P. "ribbon" mark F, 5½" high.

CHAPTER TWO: TABLE WARE

Bennington-made examples illustrated in this chapter include articles used in serving food and drink. Kitchen utensils are included in the next chapter, "Kitchen and Household Items."

Mugs, rummers, goblets, toddy cups and teapots are among the most popular collector's items in this category. Complete tea and coffee services and accessory items were made in a variety of wares, including Rockingham, flint enamel, Parian, white porcelain and graniteware. The variety of designs employed was great, making the collection of such a set today both possible and practicable.

Conspicuous by its absence is the popular "Rebecca at the Well" pattern teapot, commonly found in Rockingham and erroneously attributed to Bennington. This attractive pattern was originally made by Bennett Brothers in Baltimore, Maryland. Insofar as is known, the only examples of this pattern which ever saw Bennington are those which were brought there from other potteries. One such teapot,

which is in the possession of a descendant of the Norton family, indicates that the pattern might have been considered for production, but there is no record that it ever was produced.

At the time gold-banded white porcelain tea services were produced in quantity at Bennington, identical pieces were being made by every general pottery in this country and England. This type of ware was never marked and thus examples are impossible to identify as Bennington-made pieces without sufficient documentation. The collector will find the Bennington origin of this sort of table ware next to impossible to prove. This is also true of the graniteware fruit baskets.

Parian and blue and white porcelain plates were made in Bennington on only a very small scale, although their production in England was sizable. T. J. and J. Mayer, English makers of a "Paul and Virginia" pattern pitcher, also produced plates in large quantity; two small plates are illustrated here.

PLATE 109. Rare Flint Enamel Covered Coffee Urn. 1849-1858. Helmet-shaped cover, pewter spigot, 20½" high including cover. Mugs and goblets are shown for scale.

PLATE 110. Cupid and Psyche Pattern Sugar Bowls and Teapots. 1850-1858. *Top row:* A. Parian sugar bowl, bud-shaped finial, extremely rare, 5½″ high; B. Parian teapot, bud-shaped finial, extremely rare, 6″ high. *Bottom row:* C. and D, only known examples in solid blue porcelain. These were original household posses-sions of Thomas Bailey Aldrich's grandfather Bailey in the Court Street, Portsmouth, N. H. home, now pre-served as the Aldrich Memorial. C. Sugar bowl, cover missing, 4″ high as is; D. Teapot, finial missing, 5½″ high as is. (See also Pls. 56, 57 and 105H.)

PLATE 111. EXTREMELY RARE PARIAN TEA SET. 1847-1858. *Top row:* A. Teapot, squirrel finial, 6¼" high.

Bottom row: B. Sugar bowl, squirrel finial, 5" high; C. Creamer, matching design, 3" high.

PLATE 112. PARIAN MORNING GLORY PATTERN SUGAR BOWL AND CREAMER. 1847-1858. Rare. A. Sugar bowl, 3⅛″ high; B. Creamer, same as Pls. 114B and 114C, 2½″ high.

PLATE 113. PARIAN PANELED VINE AND FLOWER PATTERN SUGAR BOWL AND CREAMER. 1847-1858. A. Sugar bowl, flower finial, 6½″ high; B. Creamer, marked with Fenton's Works mark E, 5¼″.

PLATE 114. ASSORTED PARIAN TABLE PIECES. 1847-1858. *Top row:* A. Covered mustard pot, same as Pl. 117F, 2¾″ high. *Second row:* B. and C. Morning Glory pattern, same as Pl. 112. *Third row:* D. and E. Pond Lily pattern, same as Pls. 117D and 117G. *Bot-*tom row: F. Rare blue and white porcelain covered bowl, matching plate. Bowl, 5″ high; Plate, 7¼″ diam.; G. Parian covered bowl, matching plate. Bowl, 4″ high; Plate, 7″ diam.

PLATE 115. Rare Parian Pond Lily Pattern Cups and Saucers. 1847-1858. Similar pieces were made in England by T. J. and J. Mayer. *Top row:* A. Cup, 2½″ high, 2½″ diam.; B. Saucer, 5½″ diam. *Bottom row:* C. Cup, 2½″ high, 4″ diam.; D. Ivy pattern saucer, 6¾″ diam.

PLATE 116. Assorted Parian Table Pieces. 1847-1858. *Top row:* A. and C. Pair, bowl, 2″ high, 4¼″ diam.; B. Oval bowl, 2½″ high, 7″ long, 5″ wide; C. Bowl, 2″ high, 4¼″ diam. *Center row:* D. Plate, blue and white porcelain, also made in England, 7″ diam. *Bottom row:* E. Crocus jar, applied rose, 4″ high, 5¾″ diam.; F. Plate, pink and white porcelain, also made in England, 8″ diam.; G. Small plate, colored glazes, made by T. J. and J. Mayer, England, 3¾″ high; H. Small footed compote, applied grapes, 2½″ high, 6½″ diam.; I. Small plate, pink and white porcelain, made by T. J. and J. Mayer, England, 3¾″ diam.

PLATE 117. ASSORTED PARIAN POND LILY PATTERN TABLE PIECES. 1847-1858. *Top row:* A. Footed egg cup, 2⅛" high; B. Small bowl, 1¼" high; C. Salt shaker, 2¾" high. *Bottom row:* D. Pitcher, 3" high, same as Pl. 114E; E. Plate, 5¾" diam.; F. Covered mustard pot, 2¾" high; G. Sugar bowl, 4" high. All of these items are uncommon.

PLATE 118. ASSORTED PARIAN TABLE PIECES. 1847-1858. *Top row:* A. Pitcher, 3¼" high; B. Bowl, 2" high; C. Inkwell, masks, matches F, 1½" high. *Bottom row:* D. Pitcher, 3" high; E. Toothpick holder, 2¾" high; F. Pitcher, 3" high.

PLATE 119. GRANITEWARE FRUIT BASKETS. 1850-1858. *Top row:* Gold trim, straight lattice openwork sides, 4½″ high, 8½″ diam. *Bottom row:* B. Plain, entwined loop openwork sides, 4½″ high, 8½″ diam.

PLATE 120. PART OF A WHITE PORCELAIN TEA SERVICE. 1850-1858. Gold striping. *Top row:* A. Cake plate, 10″ by 9″ diam. *Center row:* B. Covered toddy cup, 4″ high. *Bottom row:* C. and D. Cups, 3″ high, saucers, 6½″ diam.

PLATE 121. PART OF A WHITE PORCELAIN TEA SERVICE. 1850-1858. Gold striping. A. Cup, 3″ high, 3½″ diam., saucer, 6½″ diam.; B. Pitcher, 6″ high; C. Teapot, covered, 9½″ high.

PLATE 122. PART OF A WHITE PORCELAIN TEA SERVICE. 1850-1858. Gold striping. Similar wares were produced by every sizable pottery in this country and England. Like Pls. 120 and 121, this sort of tea service is impossible to identify positively without history or documentation. *Top row:* A. Teapot, 9½″ high. *Bottom row:* B. Sugar bowl, 7½″ high; C. Pitcher, 7¾″ high.

PLATE 123. RARE ROCKINGHAM COVERED BOWL. 1844-1858, 4⅝" high, including cover, 4½" diam.

PLATE 124. EXTREMELY RARE ROCKINGHAM COVERED DISH. 1844-1858. Footed and with handles, cream color glaze inside, 7½" high, 12" long, including handles.

PLATE 125. EXTREMELY RARE FLINT ENAMEL TABLE ARTICLES. 1849-1858. *Top row:* A. Relish dish, 10″ long, 5¼″ wide. *Bottom row:* B. Covered butter dish, marked with 1849 mark A, 5¼″ high, 7½″ diam.; C. Bottle or flask, two men drinking at table, molded grapes and vine, 6″ high. Reproductions have been made in Rockingham but are coarser and heavier than the original thin-walled ones.

PLATE 126. FLINT ENAMEL SUGAR BOWLS. 1849-1858. *Top row:* A. Marked with 1849 mark A, 9⅜″ high; B. 7⅝″ high (See also Pl. 135B.). *Bottom row:* C. 5⅞″ high; D. Marked with 1849 mark A, matches Pls. 137F, 138E and 138F, 7″ high.

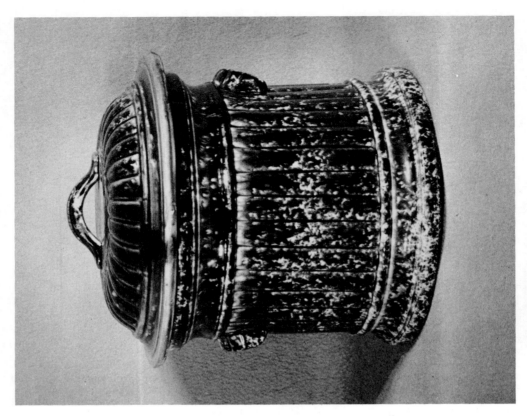

PLATE 128. COVERED ROCKINGHAM TOBACCO JAR. 1847-1858. Plain cream color glaze inside, 8½" high.

PLATE 127. COVERED TOBACCO JARS. 1847-1858. *Top row:* A. Rockingham, applied handles, Gothic arches, 10½" high. *Bottom row:* B. Flint enamel, Gothic arches, marked with 1849 mark A, 11½" high.

PLATE 130. COVERED TOBACCO JARS. 1847-1858. *Top row:* A. Rockingham, with tobacco pod finial, marked with 1849 mark A, 11¾" high; B. Same as A, marked with 1849 mark A, 10¼" high. *Bottom row:* C. Rockingham, 8½" high; D. Flint enamel, same as Pl. 129C; E. Rockingham, 8¼" high.

PLATE 129. ALTERNATE RIB PATTERN TOBACCO JARS. 1849-1858. Four sizes of the same pattern in different glazes. *Top row:* A. Rockingham, marked with extremely rare U.S.P. "oval" mark H, 9" high; B. Flint enamel, marked with 1849 mark A, 10" high. *Bottom row:* C. Flint enamel, marked with 1849 mark A, 7" high; D. Rockingham, 7¾" high.

95

PLATE 131. ROCKINGHAM BEAKERS AND GOBLETS. 1844-1858. *Top row:* A. Beaker, 3½″ high; B. Beaker, 3¼″ high. *Bottom row:* C. Goblet, 4½″ high; D. Goblet, 5¾″ high; E. Handled goblet, 4¾″ high.

PLATE 132. ROCKINGHAM FOOTED GOBLETS. 1844-1858. *Top row:* A. Handled, 3⅞″ high; B. 4″ high, rare; C. Handled, 4¾″ high. *Bottom row:* D. 4¼″ high; E. 4½″ high; F. 5½″ high; G. 5¼″ high.

PLATE 133. ROCKINGHAM BEAKERS AND MUGS. 1844-1858. *Top row:* A. Beaker, 3⅛″ high; B. Handled mug, rare shape, 4⅛″ high; C. Beaker, 3⅜″ high. *Bottom row:* D. Handled mug, 3″ high; E. Only known example of this shape, peculiarly marked with 1849 mark A, 3⅛″ high; F. Handled mug, 2⅞″ high.

PLATE 134. ROCKINGHAM HANDLED MUGS. 1844-1858. There are many variants, different handles being applied to different bodies. Similar mugs were made also by many different potteries. *Top row:* A. 4″ high; B. Only known example of this shape, peculiarly marked with 1849 mark A, 3½″ high; C. 3¼″ high; D. 3″ high. *Bottom row:* E. This design was not made at Bennington, but was a product of Bennett Bros., Baltimore, Md., 4″ high (For similar figure see toby snuff jars, Pls. 402, 417 and 418.) ; F. 4⅛″ high; G. 3⅝″ high.

97

PLATE 135. RARE COMPLETE FLINT ENAMEL TEA AND COFFEE SERVICE. 1849-1858. A. Pitcher, 5⅝" high (See also Pl. 27C.) ; B. Sugar bowl, 7⅝" high (See also Pl. 126B.) ; C. Teapot, 9" high; D. Coffeepot, 12¼" high. All marked with 1849 mark A.

PLATE 136. TWO FLINT ENAMEL COFFEEPOTS. 1849-1858. Note different placement of spout and handle on paneled body. A. Helmet cover, spout and handle on rib, 12¼" high; B. Peaked cover, spout and handle on panel, 13" high. Both marked with 1849 mark A.

PLATE 137. Flint Enamel Teapots. 1849-1858. *Top row:* A. Rare, 4¼" high; B. Extremely rare, marked with 1849 mark A, 7½" high; C. Rare, 6" high. *Bottom row:* D. 9" high (See also Pl. 135C.) ; E. Rare, 6¼" high; F. Rockingham, 8½" high (See also Pl. 138F.)

PLATE 138. Rockingham and Flint Enamel Teapots. 1844-1858. *Top row:* A. Rockingham, 7⅝" high. B. Flint enamel, 8¾" high; C. Rockingham, handle differs from A, 7⅝" high. *Bottom row:* D. Rockingham, 7" high; E. Flint enamel, alternate ribs, marked with 1849 mark A, rare size, 6½" high; F. Flint enamel, alternate ribs, marked with 1849 mark A, 7⅝" high.

PLATE 139. EXTREMELY RARE ROCKINGHAM TEAPOT. 1844-1858, Acanthus Leaf pattern, 4¾" high. (See also design on Pl. 184D.)

PLATE 140. ALTERNATE RIB PATTERN FLINT ENAMEL TEAPOT. Only known example with covered and pierced spout in this design, 1849-1858, impressed with 1849 mark A, 6¾″ high.

CHAPTER THREE: KITCHEN AND HOUSEHOLD ACCESSORIES

This chapter, which includes a miscellany of items in daily home use, shows more than any other the diversification of production at Bennington. It is hard to conceive of a common household item which was not made in either pottery or porcelain. The articles range from simple, unadorned objects, ideally suited to the specific need for which they were designed, to more elaborate objects which cannot be regarded as solely functional.

Miscellaneous household items such as washbasins with plumbing attachments, washboards, shelf brackets and tiles are difficult to find today, as their very intensive usage caused them to be broken more frequently than articles which were primarily decorative.

The Bennington potteries offered a variety of designs and materials in the household items necessary for daily hygiene. Some of the most beautiful flint enamel colorings are to be found in the washbowl and pitcher sets. The classic lines of some of the graniteware toilet sets were not excelled by any other similar items. Examples from the scroddled ware sets are quite rare.

The large scale of some of the toilet sets indicates that the potters at the Fenton Pottery must have had a high degree of technical skill and superior equipment in order to be able to produce them in quantity. These items were among the major Fenton production items, as every nineteenth-century home included one or more sets and occasional breakage necessitated frequent replacement. Complete toilet sets are scarce, but individual pieces from them are among the more common Bennington-made items to be found.

Cuspidors were also produced in quantity and marked examples are quite common. Though they are admittedly lacking in aesthetic appeal, some of the most desirable patterns in flint enamel ware can be found in these homely articles. The foot-warmers, which are interesting curiosities today, include few marked examples. These items were produced in Rockingham ware by many other potteries. Those which have a fish head or the head of an imaginary animal at the mouth were not made at Bennington; neither were those which show the impressions of bare feet.

In addition to a variety of jardinieres and flower pots, the Norton Pottery also made large garden urns decorated with molded grapevines.

In the range of lighting equipment it is interesting to note that Bennington-made items include candleholders and candlesticks, later lamp bases for sperm oil and kerosene lamps and, still later, (not illustrated) decorative accessories for gas fixtures.

It is virtually impossible to distinguish plain Rockingham and graniteware doorknobs from hundreds of similar ones produced at other potteries. Flint enamel knobs and drawer pulls can be identified from the distinctive use of color. Curtain tiebacks made of Rockingham ware are easy to identify as Bennington-made but they are not too common. It is not so simple to identify the graniteware tiebacks as Bennington production items. The flint enamel name plate is one of the items Christopher Webber Fenton submitted to the United States Patent Office when he sought to obtain a patent for his flint enamel in 1849.

PLATE 141. COMMON BROWN SLIP-WARE SHAVING MUG. 1805-1825. Applied small container inside for shaving soap, larger cup for hot water. This mug was used by Daniel Webster at French's Tavern, Hartland, Vermont. 5″ high, large opening 5½″ diam., small inside cup, 2⅝″ diam.

PLATE 142. ROCKINGHAM PIPKINS, WITH COVERS. 1847-1858. A. 6½″ high to cover, 9″ high to handle; B. 6″ high to cover, 7½″ high to handle.

PLATE 143. ROCKINGHAM, YELLOWWARE AND FLINT ENAMEL PIPKINS. 1849-1858. Primarily used for baking beans. *Top row:* A. Rockingham, marked with 1849 mark A, 7½″ high; B. Yellowware, 8″ high. *Bottom row:* C. Flint enamel, marked with 1849 mark A, 6⅝″ high to cover; D. Rockingham, 7″ high to bowl, 10¼″ high to handle; E. Flint enamel, marked with 1849 mark A, 7¼″ high to cover. All of these pipkins are uncommon.

PLATE 144. FLINT ENAMEL AND ROCKINGHAM BOWLS AND MOLDS. 1849-1858. *Top row:* A. Flint enamel, marked with 1849 mark A, 2¼″ high, 11¾″ long, 9¼″ wide; B. Flint enamel mixing bowl with lip, marked with 1849 mark A, 2½″ high, 10″ diam. *Bottom row:* C. Flint enamel Turk's Head cake mold, 3⅝″ high, 8″ diam.; D. Rockingham Turk's Head cake mold, 3½″ high, 10½″ diam. (CAUTION, compare with Pls. 147A and 147B.)

PLATE 145. ROCKINGHAM CAKE MOLDS. 1847-1867. *Top row:* A. 1½″ high, 3¾″ diam.; B. 3″ high, 8⅜″ diam.; C. 3″ high, 6¾″ diam. *Bottom row:* D. 4″ high, 9½″ diam.; E. 3½″ high, 10½″ diam.

105

PLATE 146. FLINT ENAMEL AND ROCKINGHAM PIE PLATES AND BAKING DISHES. 1849-1858. All six of these specimens are marked with the 1849 mark A. *Top row:* A. Rockingham pie plate, 9½" diam.; B. Flint enamel pie plate, 8" diam.; C. Flint enamel pie plate, 9⅜" diam. *Bottom row:* D. Rockingham serving plate, 9" long, 8⅝" wide; E. Flint enamel baker, 11¼" long, 9" wide; F. Rockingham baker, 10¼" long, 8¼" wide. If not marked, the Rockingham pieces are impossible to identify without history or documentation. (CAUTION, compare with Pls. 147A and 147B.)

PLATE 147. COMPARISON PIECES, NOTE CAREFULLY. A. Rockingham oval baker from East Liverpool, Ohio, unmarked, 11⅜" long, 8⅞" wide. Compare with B, Rockingham oval baker, impressed with Bennington 1849 mark A. Unmarked functional pieces without any distinguishing pattern cannot be attributed to Bennington without documentation.

106

PLATE 148. ROCKINGHAM KITCHEN ACCESSORIES. 1847-1867. *Top row:* A. and C. Pair, 2″ high, 3¼″ diam.; B. Mixing pitcher, 4″ high, 6″ diam. *Bottom row:* D. Bowl, 1½″ high, 5½″ diam.; E. Footed bowl, 2¾″ high, 5¼″ diam.; F. Bowl, 1¾″ high, 5¼″ diam.

PLATE 149. ROCKINGHAM MIXING BOWLS. 1847-1867. When unmarked, these utilitarian items without designs cannot be identified without factual family history or documentation. *Top row:* A. 5⅛″ high, 10⅜″ diam. *Bottom row:* B. 4″ high, 13″ diam., not counting lip; C. 5¼″ high, 14¼″ diam. (CAUTION, compare with Pls. 147A and 147B.)

PLATE 150. Common Yellowware Bowls. 1849-1858. *Top row:* A. and C. Pair of baking cups, 2⅛″ high, 3½″ diam.; B. Nappie, 9¼″ diam. *Bottom row:* D. Bowl, extremely rare example of yellowware marked with 1849 mark A, 5½″ high, 12¼″ diam.

PLATE 151. MORTAR AND PESTLES IN MORTAR OR WEDG-
WOOD WARE. 1856. Highly vitreous and clear-ringing,
these items are indistinguishable from similar items
produced in England. So far as is known, they were
never marked. Mortar, 3⅝" high, 6⅝" diam. at top.
Pestles, 7¾" long, including wooden handle.

PLATE 152. Norton Stoneware Churns. 1861-1881, marked "E. & L. P. Norton." A. 5-gallon size, 18" high, 34½" circ.; B. 4-gallon size, 17½" high, 31½" circ.

PLATE 153. Norton Stoneware Items, No Decoration. A. Beer or ale bottle, 10" high; B. Jug, unmarked, 4¼" high; C. Ink bottle, 2½" high; D. Jar, brown slip inside, 7" high; E. Cuspidor, brown slip-lined, marked "E. Norton & Co.," 1883-1894, 6¾" high; F. Stove pipe liner or tube, 5½" high; 8" diam. These were made in various sizes; G. Tester inkwell, used to test temperatures of kiln, 1½" high, 3¼" diam.

PLATE 154. Brown Slip-Covered Stoneware Pitchers. Made at the Norton Pottery. A. Miniature, 3¼" high; B. Batter pitcher, made by Edward L. Norton, inscribed in his handwriting, 9" high; C. Miniature pitcher, 3¾" high.

110

PLATE 155. Brown Slip-Covered Stoneware Items. Made at the Norton Pottery. *Top row:* A. Batter bowl, 1861-1881, marked "E. & L. P. Norton," 7" high; B. Buttertub, 5¾" high, 7" diam. *Bottom row:* C. Pitcher, 1861-1881, marked "E. & L. P. Norton," 10½" high; D. Jug with spout, tin covers, bale handle, 1883-1894, marked "E. Norton & Co.," 10" high.

PLATE 156. Brown Slip-Covered Stoneware Items. Made at the Norton Pottery. *Top row:* A. Covered bean pot, 4¾" high; B. Log Cabin bank, 5" high, 5½" long, 4" wide; C. Mug, 4" high. *Bottom row:* D. Mug, Gothic design, 4" high; E. Mug, 6" high; F. Mug, 4⅞" high. These slip-covered items were made by many potteries, and need history or documentation for positive identification.

PLATE 157. FLINT ENAMEL WASHBASIN. 1849-1858. Made to be built into house plumbing, brilliant colors of blue, green and orange, marked with 1849 mark A, 15¼" high.

PLATE 158. RARE ROCKINGHAM WASHBOARD. 1849-1858. Back plain yellow, marked with 1849 mark A; pottery section, 10½" high, 10¼" wide. The obviously fragile quality of this functional item has resulted in only a few surviving examples.

PLATE 159. ROCKINGHAM CROUP KETTLES OR INHALA-
TORS. 1847-1858. Top cover with two vents, one for
rubber tubing, 6½″ high.

113

PLATE 160. FLINT ENAMEL WATER COOLER. 1849-1858. Gothic arches, columns, brick embossed base, cover missing, should be like that in Pl. 18, marked with 1849 mark A, 16½″ high as is, 12¾″ diam.

114

PLATE 161. ROCKINGHAM WATER COOLERS. 1845-1867. A. Extremely rare example, marked with Fenton's Works mark E, 19½" high with cover, 16" high without cover, 11" top diam.; B. Extremely rare example with Acanthus Leaf decoration, top missing, 12¾" high, 13¼" diam., at top.

PLATE 162. GRANITEWARE SHAVING MUGS. 1850 - 1858. Owner's name in gold on all four specimens. *Top row:* A. Low foot, 4" high to rim; B. High foot, dated on cup "1854-1858," 4¾" to rim. *Bottom row:* C. Paneled, 3½" high; D. Gold flower decoration, 3½" high.

PLATE 163. ROCKINGHAM AND GRANITEWARE SOAP DISHES. 1847-1858. *Top row:* A. Graniteware, three-piece, removable liner, 4½" high, 5¼" long; B. Graniteware, three-piece, removable liner, 4" high, 5½" long.

Bottom row: C. Rockingham, same as Pl. 164D; D. Rockingham, one-piece, 2⅝" high, 5¾" long; E. Rockingham, one-piece, 2⅓" high, 4" diam.

PLATE 164. ROCKINGHAM AND FLINT ENAMEL SOAP DISHES AND TOILET BOXES. 1847-1858. *Top row:* A. Rockingham, one-piece, 2¼" high, 6¼" long, 4¾" wide; B. Flint enamel toilet box, Alternate Rib pattern, marked with 1849 mark A, two-piece, 3⅛" high, 7¾" long, 3" wide; C. Rockingham, one-piece, 3" high, 5" long, 3½" wide. *Bottom row:* D. Rockingham, one-piece, 1½" high, 4½" long, 3" wide; E. Flint enamel, three-piece, removable liner, marked with 1849 mark A, 4" high, 5⅞" long, 4½" wide; F. Rockingham, round, one-piece, 2½" high, 4" diam.

PLATE 165. FLINT ENAMEL SOAP DISHES AND TOILET BOXES. 1849-1859, marked with 1849 mark A. *Top row:* A. Two-piece, 3¾″ high, 7¾″ long, 3½″ wide; B. Three-piece, removable liner, 4″ high, 4¾″ long, 4½″ wide. *Bottom row:* C. Two-piece, Alternate Rib pattern, 4″ high, 5⅛″ long, 4″ wide; D. Two-piece, Alternate Rib pattern, 3″ high, 7½″ long, 2¾″ wide.

PLATE 166. Flint Enamel Diamond Pattern Washbowl and Pitcher. 1849-1858. Brilliantly-colored oranges, yellows and greens, marked with 1849 mark A.
A. Bowl, 4⅜" high, 13" diam.; B. Pitcher, 10½" high.

PLATE 167. Flint Enamel Scalloped Rib Pattern
Washbowl and Pitcher. 1849-1858. Brilliant colors of
brown, blue and orange, marked with 1849 mark A.
A. Twelve-sided bowl, 4¾" high, 15" diam.; B. Pitcher,
scalloped top, indented panels between bulbous ribs,
12½" high.

118

PLATE 168. Flint Enamel Scroll Edge Washbowl
and Pitcher. 1849-1858. A. Bowl, 4½" high, 14" diam.;
B. Pitcher, 12" high.

PLATE 169. Flint Enamel Alternate Rib Pattern
Washbowl and Pitcher. 1849-1858, marked with 1849
mark A. A. Bowl, 4⅛" high, 13½" diam.; B. Pitcher,
12½" high.

PLATE 170. Extremely Rare Scroddled Ware Wash-bowl and Pitcher. 1853-1858. All items in this ware are rare. A. Bowl, twelve-sided, plain pattern, marked with U.S.P. "oval" mark H, 4¼" high, 13½" diam. B. Pitcher, Diamond pattern, 10⅞" high. (See also Pls. 31, 38B and 166B.)

120

PLATE 171. GRANITEWARE GOLD-DECORATED WASH-BOWL AND PITCHER. 1850-1858. A. Bowl, plain, owner's name in gold, 14″ diam.; B. Pitcher, molded scroll under lip, owner's name in gold, 11½″ high.

PLATE 172. GRANITEWARE GOLD- AND BLUE-DECORATED WASHBOWL AND PITCHER. 1850-1858. Gothic petal molded around base. A. Bowl, owner's name in gold, blue and gold bands, 14″ diam.; B. Pitcher, owner's name in gold, blue and gold bands and scrolls, 12″ high. (See also Pls. 173 and 176.)

PLATE 173. GRANITEWARE GOLD- AND BLUE-DECORATED TOILET SET. 1850-1858. Part of a fourteen-piece toilet set, each piece marked with owner's name in gold, with blue and gold bands and scrolls. (Compare slop jar decoration with the more ornate type shown on the jar in Pl. 176.)

122

PLATE 174. GRANITEWARE DECORATED CHAMBER POTS. 1850-1858. A. Owner's name and bands in gold, 9¾" high with cover, 6" high without cover; B. Owner's name in gold, blue and gold decoration, 9¼" high with cover, 5⅞" high without cover.

PLATE 175. FLINT ENAMEL CHAMBER POT AND BED-PANS. 1849-1858, marked with 1849 mark A. *Top row:* A. Scalloped Rib pattern, 8¾" high. *Bottom row:* B. 6¼" high, 16¾" long; C. 6" high, 15" long.

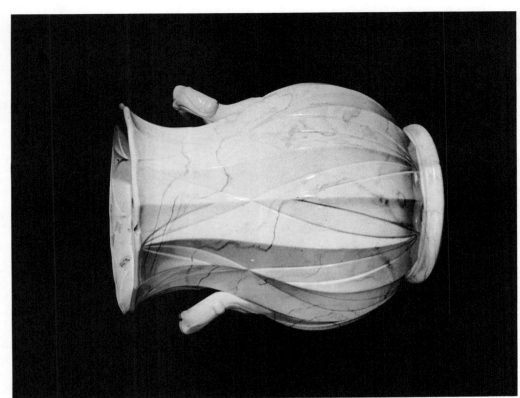

PLATE 177. Extremely Rare Scroddled Ware Diamond Pattern Slop Jars. 1853-1858. Cover missing, applied scroll handles, marked with U.S.P. "oval" mark H, 10¼" high.

PLATE 176. Graniteware Gold- and Blue-Decorated Slop Jar. Made for use by Christopher W. Fenton and family, molded Gothic petal design at bottom of cover and jar outlined in gold, 17¼" high. (See also Pl. 173.)

124

PLATE 178. Rare Flint Enamel Scalloped Rib Pattern Slop Jars. 1849-1858. Both covers missing. A. Olive-green and dark blue, plain applied handles, 10¼" high; B. Light green, orange and blue, plain applied handles, 9¼" high.

PLATE 179. Rare Rockingham Slop Jar and Bowl. 1856-1858. No underglaze, crudely finished. A. Slop jar, cover missing, applied scroll handles, 14" high; B. Bowl, large size, 6½" high, 16" diam.

PLATE 180. FLINT ENAMEL SCALLOPED RIB PATTERN FOOT BATHS. 1848-1858, marked with 1849 mark A. A. 8½" high, 20" long handle to handle, 14" wide; B. 7½" high, 16" long handle to handle, 12" wide.

PLATE 181. GRANITEWARE DECORATED FOOT BATHS. 1859-1858. A. Gold and blue decoration, owner's name and decoration in gold, 9½" high, open top 16" long, 11½" wide. B. Owner's name and decoration in gold, 9½" high, open top 16" long, 11½" wide.

126

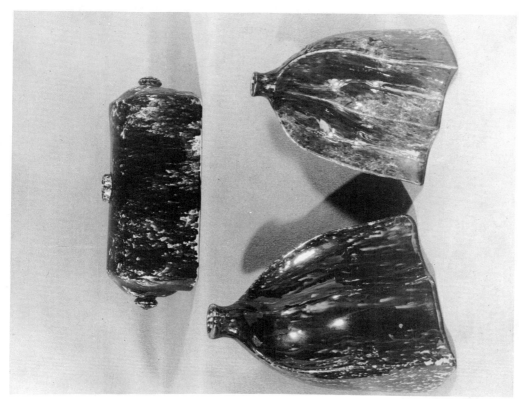

PLATE 183. Rockingham and Flint Enamel Foot Warmers. 1847-1858. These were filled either with hot water or hot sand and put under the bed covers. *Top row:* A. Rockingham, 5″ high, 12½″ long. *Bottom row:* B. Rockingham, 11″ high; C. Flint enamel, 9″ high.

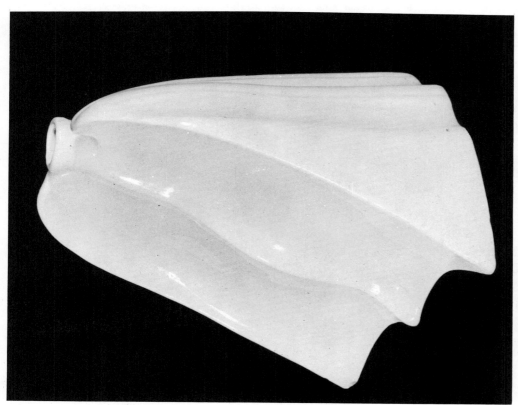

PLATE 182. Extremely Rare Graniteware Foot Warmer. 1850-1858. Only known example in this material with 1849 mark A incised on bottom, 8¾″ high.

127

PLATE 184. FLINT ENAMEL AND ROCKINGHAM CUS-
PIDORS. 1847-1858. *Top row:* A. Flint enamel, Diamond
pattern, 4½″ high, 6¼″ diam., at top; B. Rockingham,
Shell pattern, to 1867 at least, 3½″ high, 5¼″ diam.,
at top. *Bottom row:* C. Rockingham, 4⅞″ high, 8½″
diam.; D. Rockingham, Acanthus Leaf pattern, marked
with 1849 mark A, 5¾″ high, 8¼″ diam., at top.

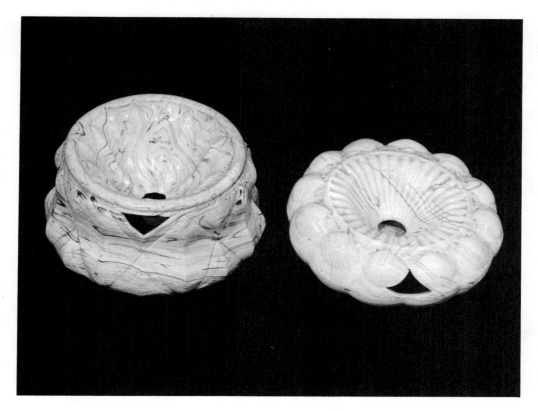

PLATE 186. EXTREMELY RARE SCRODDLED WARE CUS-PIDORS. 1853-1858. All items in this material are extremely rare. A. Diamond pattern, 5″ high, 8½″ diam., at top (See also Pl. 184A) ; B. Shell pattern, 3½″ high, 8″ diam.

PLATE 187. COMPARISON PIECES, NOTE CAREFULLY. A. Flint enamel cuspidor, impressed on bottom, "ETRURIA WORKS, 1852, EAST LIVERPOOL," 3¾″ high, 7″ diam., at bottom. Compare with B, flint enamel cuspidor, impressed on bottom with Bennington 1849 mark A, 3⅝″ high, 7¾″ diam., at bottom. Unmarked cuspidors must be cautiously attributed to Bennington.

(See opposite page.)
PLATE 185. ROCKINGHAM AND FLINT ENAMEL CUS-PIDORS. 1847-1861. *Top row:* A. Rockingham, Diamond pattern, 6¾″ high, 9½ diam., at top. B. Rockingham, Scalloped Rib pattern, 5½″ high, 8¾″ diam., at top. Only known example inscribed in script on bottom underglaze, "Manufactured by T. A. Hutchins & Co., Bennington, Vt. 1861." *Bottom row:* C. Flint enamel, only known example marked with rare 1849 mark D, 4¼″ high, 7½″ diam., at top; D. Rare mark and size, Rockingham, raised applied letters on bottom "FEN-TON'S WORKS, Bennington, Vt." in a large circle, 4⅞″ high, 11″ diam. at top; E. Flint enamel, marked with 1849 mark A, 4″ high, 6″ diam. at top. (CAUTION, compare with Pls. 187A and 187B.)

PLATE 189. ROCKINGHAM JARDINIERES. 1847-1894. Made in two parts; base 4½" high; top 6"; assembled, 11" high.

PLATE 188. ROCKINGHAM AND FLINT ENAMEL JARDINIERES. 1847-1858. Made in two parts. *Top row:* A. Base, 5⅛" high; top 7¼" high; assembled 12" high. *Bottom row:* B. Flint enamel Swirled Alternate Rib pattern, marked with 1849 mark A; base, 4" high; top, 7⅛" high; assembled, 10¼" high; C. Flint enamel base only, 4" high.

130

PLATE 191. BROWN SLIP-COVERED FLOWER POTS. 1867-1894. These were made in many varieties (See Fig. VIII). *Top row*: A. 4¾" high; B. 5⅞" high. *Bottom row*: C. 6¾" high; D. 6" high.

PLATE 190. ROCKINGHAM JARDINIERES. 1847-1894. Made in two parts. *Top row*: A. Dark, base, 3¾" high; top, 8⅜" high; assembled, 11" high. *Bottom row*: B. Base, 4⅛" high; top, 6½" high; assembled, 9¾" high; C. Base, 4½" high; top, 6½" high; assembled, 10" high.

PLATE 192. Rare Biscuit-Fired Scroll Support. 1847-1858. Used to hold up a shelf or as a mantel support, 10″ high, 5¼″ wide, 2¾″ deep. (Compare with finished fired specimen.)

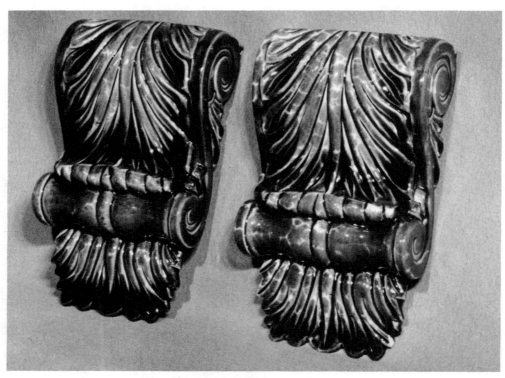

PLATE 193. Extremely Rare Flint Enamel Scroll Supports. 1849-1858. Rare olive-green color. A. 10¼″ long, 5½″ wide; B. 10″ long, 5¾″ wide.

PLATE 194. RARE FLINT ENAMEL TILES AND CEILING DECORATION. 1849-1858. *Top row:* A. Olive-green, marked with 1849 mark A, 7″ square; B. Extremely rare gray-purple, 8½″ long, 7″ wide. *Bottom row:* C. Rockingham ceiling decoration, only known example, 5¾″ high, 9¼″ diam.

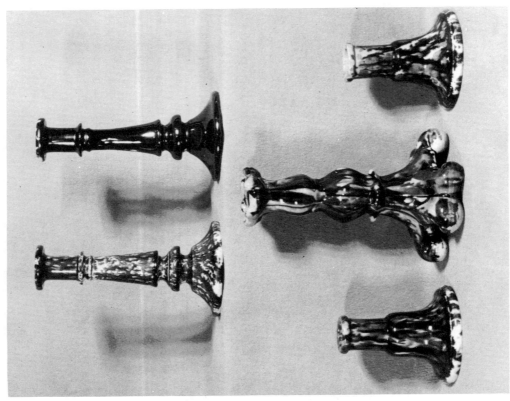

PLATE 196. ROCKINGHAM AND FLINT ENAMEL CANDLE-
sticks. 1849-1858. *Top row:* A. Rockingham, 8⅛" high;
B. Rockingham, 8" high. *Bottom row:* C. Flint enamel,
4½" high; D. Flint enamel, 8¼" high; E. Flint enamel,
4¼" high.

PLATE 195. RARE FLINT ENAMEL DISH CANDLEHOLDERS.
1849-1858. *Top row:* A. 3½" high, 4⅞" diam. *Bottom
row:* B. 3½" high, 6½" diam.

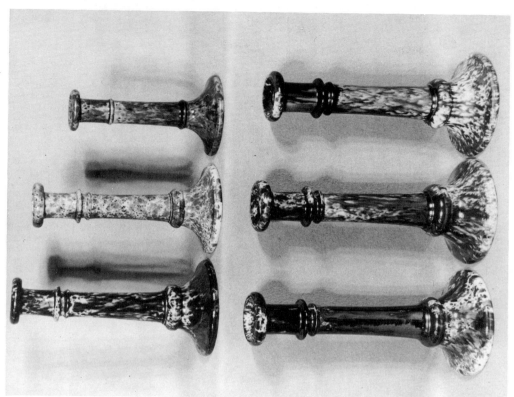

PLATE 198. ROCKINGHAM AND FLINT ENAMEL CANDLE-STICKS. 1849-1858. *Top row:* A. Rockingham, 9⅛″ high; B. Flint enamel, 8½″ high; C. Flint enamel, 6⅞″ high. *Bottom row:* D. Flint enamel, 9⅞″ high; E. Flint enamel, 9¾″ high; F. Rockingham, 9⅜″ high.

PLATE 197. ROCKINGHAM AND FLINT ENAMEL CANDLE-STICKS. 1849-1858. *Top row:* A. Rockingham, 7½″ high; B. Rockingham, 7¼″ high. *Bottom row:* C. Flint enamel, 7¾″ high; D. Flint enamel, 9″ high; E. Flint enamel, 9⅜″ high.

PLATE 199. Door Knobs and Drawer Pulls. 1847-1867. All measurements are diameter. *Top row:* A. Pair, flint enamel, 2¼"; B. Rockingham, 1¾"; C. Pair, door knobs, 2¼". *Second row:* D. Rockingham, 2"; E. Rockingham drawer pull, 1⅜"; F. Flint enamel, 1¾". *Third row:* G. Flint enamel, light, 2⅛"; H. Flint enamel, light, 1⅝"; I. Rockingham door knob, 2½"; J. Rockingham, upside down, 2¼". *Bottom row:* K. Rockingham, 2¼"; L. Flint enamel, 2¼".

PLATE 200. Rare Flint Enamel and Rockingham Curtain Tie-Backs. 1849-1858. All four are 4½" long and 4" in diameter. A, C and D are flint enamel, B is Rockingham.

136

PLATE 201. EXTREMELY RARE PARIAN CURTAIN TIE-BACKS. 1847-1858. *Top row:* A. Top view of C, flower design, 3¾" diam.; B. Top view of D, swirl design, 3½" diam. *Bottom row:* C. Side view of A, 3⅝" long; D. Side view of B, 3⅜" long.

PLATE 202. GRANITEWARE ACCESSORIES. 1850-1858. *Top row:* Curtain tie-back, cobalt blue decoration, 4" diam.; B. Name plate, decorated with purple, green and gold, 7" long, 3¾" high (See also Pl. 206); C: Curtain tie-back, outer band blue, center gold, 4" diam. *Bottom row:* D. Keyhole escutcheon, gold decoration, 3⅝" high, 2½" wide; E. Keyhole cover, matches B, 2¾" long; F. Door knob escutcheon, gold decoration, 2½" diam.; G. Keyhole escutcheon, blue flowers, gold leaves, 3⅝" high, 2½" wide.

137

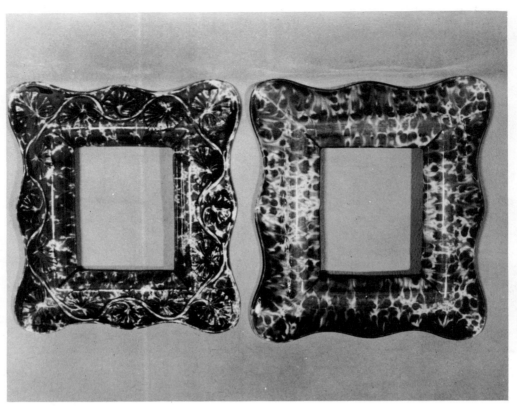

PLATE 204. FLINT ENAMEL PICTURE FRAMES. 1849-1858. A. Scalloped edge, plain, 12" high, 9½" wide; B. Extremely rare Ivy Vine pattern, 11¾" high, 9" wide (See also Fig. VII.)

PLATE 203. ROCKINGHAM AND FLINT ENAMEL NAME PLATES. 1847-1858. Made to be attached to doors. *Top row:* A. Rockingham, 6¼" long, 3¼" high. *Second row:* B. Flint enamel, 7" long, 3¼" high. *Third row:* C. Rockingham, 7¼" long, 3¼" high. *Bottom row:* D. Flint enamel, shield shape, 8" long, 3¾" high.

138

PLATE 206. PARIAN NAME PLATES AND ALPHABET LETTERS. 1847-1858. *Top row*: A. Molded grape design, 7″ long, 3¾″ high. (See also Pl. 202B.) *Center row*: B. Molded flower design, 7¾″ long, 4″ high. *Bottom row*: C. Assorted alphabet letters to be used in name plates.

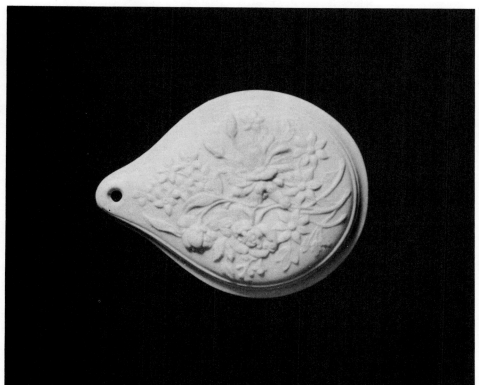

PLATE 205. EXTREMELY RARE PARIAN KEYHOLE COVER. 1847-1858. Pear-shaped, finely molded flower detail, 4¾″ high, 3½″ wide.

PLATE 207. Extremely Rare Flint Enamel Lamp
Base. 1849-1858. One of the few examples of 3″ high
base, dark browns and blue, marked with 1849 mark A,
20″ over-all height, including original glass.

PLATE 208. Rare Flint Enamel Lamp Base. 1849-1858. Pedestal light green, base brown, glass original, marked with 1849 mark A, base 9″ high, over-all 24″ high.

SECTION II: FANCY ARTICLES

————•————

CHAPTER FOUR: VASES, EWERS, COLOGNE BOTTLES AND TRINKET BOXES

Any vase not included among these illustrations (or in the group of miniature vases under Chapter Seven, "Novelty Items") should have a traceable history in order to document its Bennington origin before it is accepted as a product from Fenton's Pottery. A few patterns were made in Rockingham, flint enamel and the extremely rare scroddled ware. However, by far the largest two groups of vases produced under Christopher Webber Fenton's direction at Bennington were made in Parian and blue and white porcelain.

Similar vases decorated with applied grapes, leaves and tendrils were made in quantity by various English manufacturers during the same period as they were being produced in Bennington. Such vases were never marked, and unless photographs of known Bennington-made vases can be used for comparison, positive identification is difficult if not impossible. All known examples are illustrated, but there is no claim advanced that this group includes one of every single pattern made.

In every illustration the size of the vase has been listed. Attention should be given to the variations in size within the same pattern; it was a common practice to manufacture the same pattern in at least three sizes and, in many instances, as many as six or seven. Of course not all the possible variations in size can be included here.

As a general rule, variations in color are more prevalent among the vases made at Bennington than in any other production items. The pink and white porcelain vases were a rare production item, yet the pattern is to be found in both Parian and blue and white porcelain. The use of pink as a basic color never passed the experimental stage, and such items were produced in limited quantities only. It has not yet been established that pink and white porcelain articles ever reached the mass production stage. The technical difficulties of higher firing temperatures needed for pink finishes would naturally limit production.

Experimentation in applying various colors to a biscuit piece and refiring it with an inside glaze seems to have been almost entirely limited to vases. The use of gold decoration on Parian ware is to be found only on vases and trinket boxes. Many combinations of gold and color are to be found on vases, with different combinations applied even to the same pattern.

There was much intermingling of elements of one pattern with parts of others and a further mixture of Parian patterns with the colored porcelains. Several different tops and handles were used with a basic mold, plus the varied use of the ever-present applied grapes. A vase could easily be made into a ewer by the addition of a lip and a single handle.

In a few instances the same basic mold was adapted in more than one material for both a ewer and a cologne bottle. Cologne bottles are much rarer than the trinket boxes, and bottles with matching stoppers are doubly rare. Caution should be exercised in identifying them as Bennington-made, as similar articles are known to have been made in England and France during the decade of the 1850's.

With few exceptions these decorative items were made in either Parian or blue and white porcelain. While more than 130 patterns are known to have been used in making trinket boxes at Bennington, the variations in decorating them are almost as limitless as in the case of the vases. Various applied ornaments —grapes, leaves and tendrils and occasionally flowers—were used.

As with the vases, the same pattern was made in trinket boxes in both Parian and blue and white porcelain. In the case of a distinctive blue and white porcelain pattern, it is not at all uncommon to find the decorative color located differently on different pieces. Experimentation was made at Bennington to a small extent with colors other than blue, including the tans used in some of the pitchers. Only one example is known in which a salmon-pink glaze was used. The rare gray-blue shade associated with the Eng-

lish modeler John Harrison during his stay in Bennington, appears in one example of a trinket box. (This color is also found on his special-order flower pieces.)

Because size is not a primary identification feature in the case of trinket boxes, all of which are obviously small, this information has been omitted from these captions. There is no known example of a marked Bennington-made trinket box or cologne bottle. A plausible reason has been suggested for this omission: that any mark was deliberately left off so that these American-made ornamental items, which closely resembled their European counterparts, might be as readily accepted in the market as the more popular English-made ones.

PLATE 209. EXTREMELY RARE PARIAN COLOGNE BOTTLE. 1847-1858. Very fine applied grapes, leaves on cover, 8½″ high.

PLATE 210. TWO CRUDE VASES OR SPILL-HOLDERS. 1847-1850. A. Graniteware, only positively identified example in this shape, 6″ high; B. Blue and white porcelain, only known example, 5″ high.

PLATE 211. GRANITEWARE BANDED VASES. 1850-1858. A. Only known example, white with gold and blue bands, sides slightly concave, 4¾″ high; B. Only known example, gold and plum bands, flaring lip, 5½″ high.

144

PLATE 212. RARE ROCKINGHAM AND FLINT ENAMEL VASES. 1849-1858. *Top row:* A. and C. Pair, Rockingham, 3½″ high; B. Flint enamel, impressed with extremely rare 1849 mark C, 6¼″ high. *Bottom row:* D. and F. Pair, dark Rockingham, impressed with 1849 mark A, 8½″ high; E. Flint enamel, impressed with 1849 mark A, 11¼″ high.

PLATE 213. FLINT ENAMEL TULIP VASES. 1849-1858. *Top row:* A, B, C, 9″ high. *Bottom row:* E. 9″ high; D. and F. 9⅞″ high. These vases are among the most sought-after pieces, closely resembling the Sandwich glass vases of the same type.

PLATE 214. EXTREMELY RARE TULIP VASES. 1849-1858.
A. Graniteware, 10″ high; B. Flint enamel, small size,
8½″ high; C. Scroddled ware, 10″ high.

PLATE 215. SCRODDLED WARE COTTAGE-TYPE VASE.
1853-1858. Only known example, beautiful dark browns
and reds on cream background, 8″ high.

PLATE 216. EXTREMELY RARE COTTAGE-TYPE VASES. 1850-1858. *Top row:* A. and D. Pair, miniature, blue and white porcelain, molded grapes, 2½" high; B. Blue and white porcelain, molded grapes, 5½" high; C. Parian, applied grapes, 5½" high. *Bottom row:* E. Blue and white porcelain, two bunches of applied grapes, 7¼" high (See also G.) ; F. Blue and white porcelain, four bunches of applied grapes, 8½" high; G. Blue and white porcelain, four bunches of applied grapes, 7¼" high. (Compare E, F, G with Pls. 218A and 218B.)

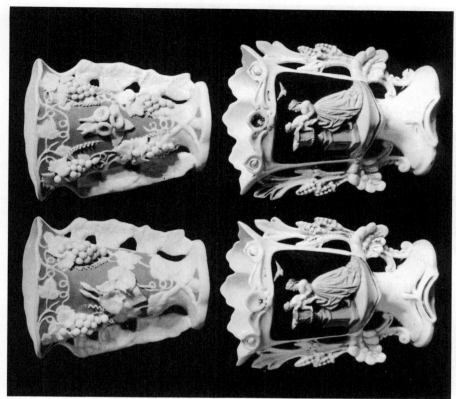

PLATE 218. EXTREMELY RARE COTTAGE-TYPE VASES. 1850-1858. *Top row:* A. Blue and white porcelain, two bunches of applied grapes, back is plain white, 7" high; B. Blue and white porcelain, four bunches of applied grapes, back is plain white, 7" high. (Compare A and B with Pls. 216E, 216F and 216G.) *Bottom row:* C. and D. Only known marked pair of cottage-type vases in glazed white porcelain. Figures in oranges, turquoise, on a brown background, trimmed in gold. On back is marked in gold, "U.S.P. Co., Bennington, Vt.," 7½" high. (Compare with Pl. 217.)

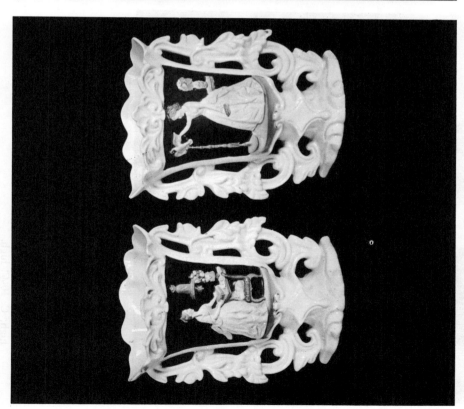

PLATE 217. EXTREMELY RARE COTTAGE-TYPE VASES. 1850-1858. A. Pink dress, brown background, gold trimmings, 5¾" high; B. Blue dress, brown background, gold trimmings, 5¾" high. These two designs, plus Pls. 218C and 218D, are the only designs of this type known to have been made in the Bennington pottery.

149

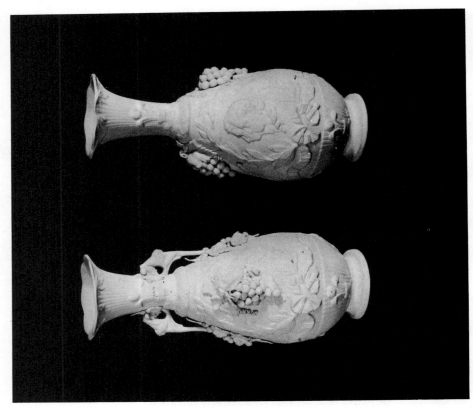

PLATE 220. Parian Porcelain Vases, Victoria and Albert Pattern. 1850-1858. A. With applied grapes, 11″ high; B. Portrait medallion, 11″ high.

PLATE 219. Blue and White Porcelain Vases, Victoria and Albert Pattern. 1850-1858. Extremely rare pattern, made also in Parian. (See Pl. 220.) Originally included portrait medallion, as in Pl. 220B. When before the Civil War Southern and Northern sentiments clashed over England's trade policies, the portraits on existing vases were covered up with applied grapes, as in C and Pl. 220A, and the portraits were then cut from the mold, as in A and B. A. 7½″ high; B. 9″ high; C. 10½″ high.

150

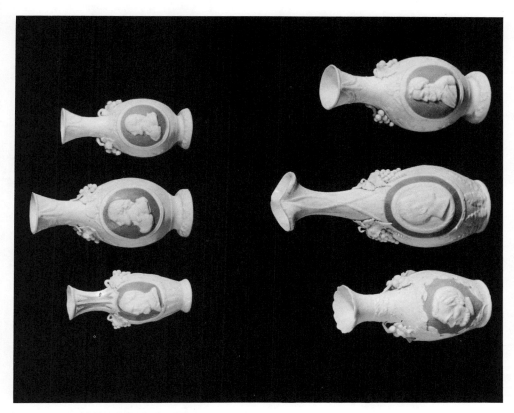

PLATE 222. BLUE AND WHITE PORCELAIN VASES, POR-
TRAIT MEDALLION. 1850-1858. *Top row:* A. 6" high;
B. 8" high; C. 6¾" high. *Bottom row:* D. Lincoln, 7¼"
high; E. 10¼" high; F. Lincoln, 8" high.

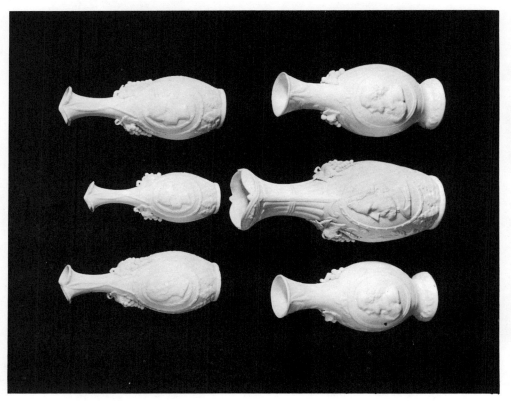

PLATE 221. PARIAN PORCELAIN VASES, PORTRAIT ME-
DALLION. 1847-1858. *Top row:* A. and C. Pair, 8" high,
Victoria on one side, Albert on reverse, of each vase;
B. Same as A and C, 7" high. (Compare A, B and C
with Pl. 222E.) *Bottom row:* D. 8¼" high; E. 10½"
high; F. 8½" high. (Compare difference in height with
D. See also Pls. 222B, 222C and 222F.)

151

PLATE 223. EXTREMELY RARE PAIR OF PINK AND WHITE PORCELAIN VASES. 1850-1858, 7½″ high. The pink is colored similarly to the method used for coloring the blue porcelain and has a similar thickness.

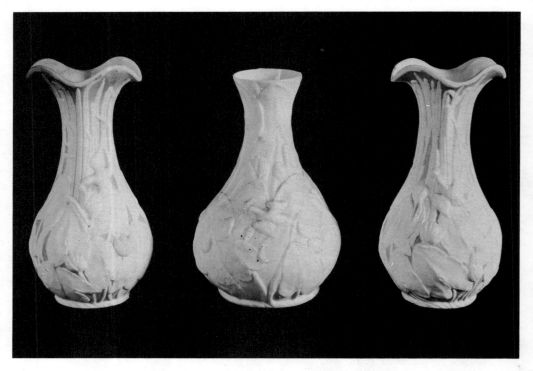

PLATE 224. EXTREMELY RARE PAIR OF GREEN AND WHITE PORCELAIN VASES. 1850-1858. A. and C. Green and white porcelain, 7¼″ high; B. Parian, similar design, 7″ high. The top of this specimen has obviously been ground off.

PLATE 225. EXTREMELY RARE "BELLEEK"-TYPE POR-CELAIN VASES. 1850-1858. Only a few pieces are known to have been made in this experimental glaze. (See Pls. 324H and 401A.) *Top row:* A. and B. Pair, 6¼" high. (See also Pls. 230B, 260I, 287B, 287H and 307.) *Bottom row:* C. and D. 6¼" high. (See also Pl. 227H.)

PLATE 226. Parian Body Vase with Colored Glazes. 1850-1858, only known example of this extremely rare pattern, with colored glaze, 8½″ high. The eagle is brown with red mouth and black tongue, the top scallops are dark green, with light green pendant leaves. It rests on a yellow pedestal with scrolls in red and green. The trefoil decoration above the eagle is red on top, shading to yellow pendant. (See also Pl. 280A.)

154

PLATE 227. PARIAN BODY VASES WITH COLORED GLAZES. 1850-1858. A. and C. Pair with figures colored, hair on both figures dark gray, with clothes in pastel yellows, pinks and greens, 4⅝" high; B. Parian, without colors, 4⅝" high. (See also Pl. 248E.)

PLATE 228. PARIAN BODY VASES. 1847-1858. *Top row:* A. Green glaze applied, rare, 9¾" high; B. Brown glaze applied, rare, 9¾" high. *Bottom row:* Blue and white porcelain, 6¼" high; D. Parian, 7½" high; E. Parian, 6¼" high. (See also Pls. 64, 103, 232E, 251, 276G and 290.)

PLATE 229. PARIAN BODY VASES WITH APPLIED COLOR. 1850-1858. Extremely rare examples of fired-on color used on a Parian body. *Top row:* A. and B. Pair, 8¾" high, with dark green ivy leaves and red-orange ber-ries. *Bottom row:* C. and E. Pair, 6½" high; D. 8½" high. C, D and E all have light blue-green leaves with buds in light pink and yellow, shiny glaze. (See also Pls. 231A, 292E, 292F, 292G and 292H.)

157

PLATE 230. PARIAN PORCELAIN VASES, COLORED DEC-
ORATION. 1847-1858. All five of these pieces have had
the color applied after the biscuit firing. *Top row:*
A. Purple grapes, green leaves, 5¼" high; B. Ewer,
pink inside, bright red outlined leaves, light green
shield, 6½" high (See also Pls. 225, 225A, 225B, 260I,
287B, 287H and 307J.) *Bottom row:* C. Green leaves,
6½" high; D. Transfer flowers, gold leaves and grapes,
7½" high; E. Green leaves, purple grapes, 7¼" high.

158

PLATE 231. Blue and White Porcelain Vases with Gold Decoration. 1850-1858. *Top row:* A. Gold grapes and leaf edges, 9¾″ high (See also Pls. 229C, 229D, 229E, 292C, 292F, 292G and 292H.) ; B. Gold grapes and leaf edges, 7″ high. (See also Pls. 268A, 268B, 268C, 289D, 289E, 289F, 289G and 289H.) *Bottom row:* C. Gold polka-dots and ten-pointed star, 9″ high; D. Light blue and red-orange polka-dots, 8″ high. (See also Pls. 291H, 291I and 291J.) All four of these vases are uncommon.

159

PLATE 232. BLUE AND WHITE PORCELAIN VASES. 1850-1858. Bottom three have added gold decoration. *Top row:* A. and C. Pair, 9½" high; B. 8⅞" high. *Bottom row:* D. and F. Pair, with grapes, leaf edges and top loopings in gold, rare, 10¾" high; E. Parian body with grapes, leaves, handles and neck edge in gold, rare, 6⅝" high. (See also Pls. 64, 103C, 228, 251, 276G and 290.)

PLATE 233. BLUE AND WHITE PORCELAIN VASE, AP-
PLIED DECORATION. 1850-1858. Only known example
with so many fine applied flowers, perhaps a presentation piece, 10¼" high.

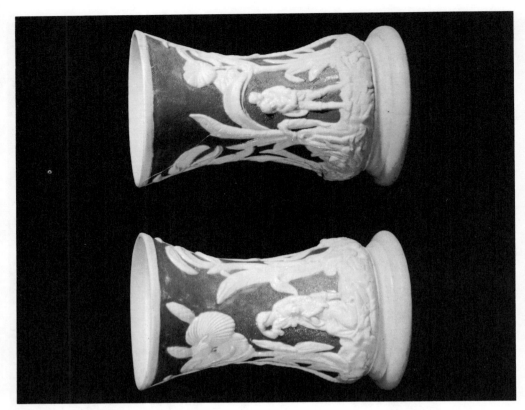

PLATE 235. BLUE AND WHITE PORCELAIN VASES, PAUL AND VIRGINIA PATTERN. 1850-1858. Extremely rare shape, marked with U.S.P. "ribbon" mark F, 8¾" high. This pattern was also made in pitchers. (See Pls. 76 and 77A.)

PLATE 234. UNIQUE PAUL AND VIRGINIA PATTERN VASE. 1853-1858. Made of red clay, unglazed outside, brown slip inside, outside covered with a crude, cream-colored slip, marked with U.S.P. "ribbon" mark F, 9⅝" high.

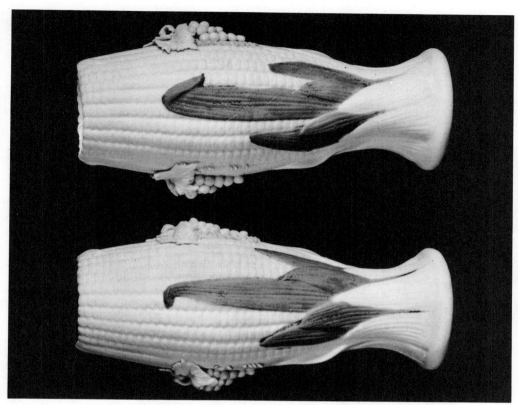

PLATE 237. BLUE AND WHITE PORCELAIN VASES, EAR
OF CORN DESIGN. 1850-1858. A. and B. Pair, extremely
rare with blue leaves, applied grapes, 8½" high. (See
also Pl. 291D.)

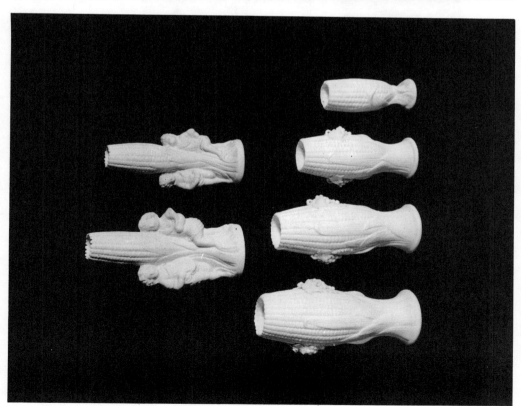

PLATE 236. PARIAN PORCELAIN VASES, EAR OF CORN
DESIGN. 1847-1858. One of the few strictly American
motifs. *Top row:* A. Uncommon, 9" high; B. Uncommon, 7½" high. *Bottom row:* C. With grapes, 8½"
high; D. With grapes, 7½" high; E. With grapes, 6¼"
high; F. Without grapes, 4¾" high.

163

PLATE 238. Parian Porcelain Vases, Figures. 1847-1858. A. 8¾″ high; B. 6½″ high; C. 8″ high.

PLATE 239. PARIAN PORCELAIN VASES, FIGURES. 1847-1858. *Top row:* A. Pair with B, 7⅛" high; B. Pair with A, 7⅜" high. *Bottom row:* C. and D. Pair, both 9½" high. These two pairs were inspired by similar Staffordshire designs, and are difficult to identify positively without personal history.

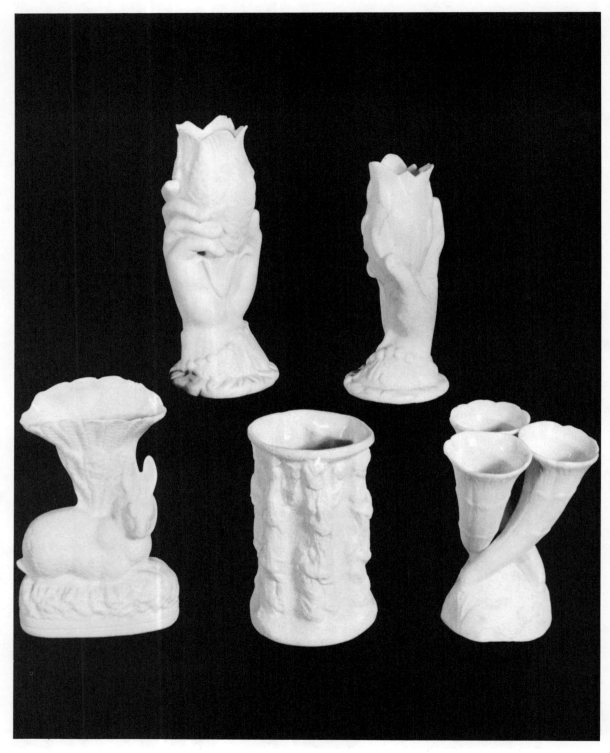

PLATE 240. PARIAN PORCELAIN VASES, HANDS. 1847-1858. *Top row:* A. Right hand, 6" high; B. Right hand, 5¼" high. *Bottom row:* C. 5¼" high; D. 4¼" high; E. 4¼" high.

PLATE 241. PARIAN PORCELAIN VASES, HANDS. 1847-1858. *Top row:* A. Right hand, 4¼″ high; B. and C. Pair, left and right hands, extremely rare, 6½″ high; D. 4¼″ high. *Center row:* E. Right hand, 7¾″ high.

(See also Pl. 243A.) *Bottom row:* F. and G. Pair, left and right hands, extremely rare, 8¼″ high. (See model for right hand vase, Fig. XII.)

PLATE 242. PARIAN PORCELAIN VASES, HANDS. 1847-1850. *Top row:* A. Left hand, 5¼" high; B. Right hand, 8¼" high; C. Right hand, 6" high. *Center row:* D. Left hand, 4" high; E. Right hand, 2" high; F. Right hand, 3½" high. *Bottom row:* G. Right hand, 3" high; H. Right hand, 3¼" high; I. Right hand, 3¼" high; J. Right hand, 3" high.

PLATE 243. Parian Porcelain Vases, Hands. 1847-
1858. *Top row:* A. Gold-decorated, right hand, 7¾″
high. (See also Pl. 241E.) *Center row:* B. and C. Duplicates, right hand, 8″ high. *Bottom row:* D. and F.
Duplicates, right hand, raised, glazed polka-dots which
were originally covered with gold leaf, 8½″ high; E.
Right hand holding shell with gold-covered, raised,
glazed polka-dots, 6″ high.

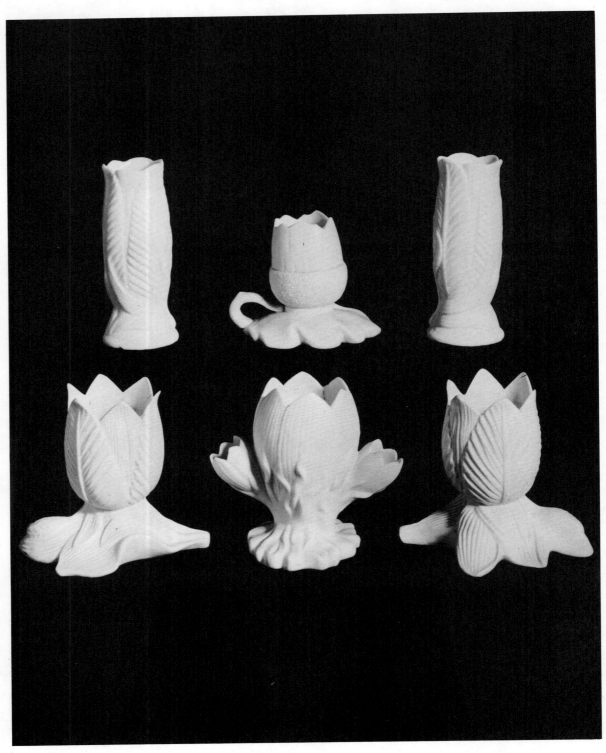

PLATE 244. PARIAN PORCELAIN VASES. 1847-1858. *Top row:* A. and C. Pair, 5⅜″ high; B. Acorn, 3¾″ high. *Bottom row:* D. and F. Pair, 4⅞″ high; E. Crocus, 5″ high. All four of these designs are rare.

170

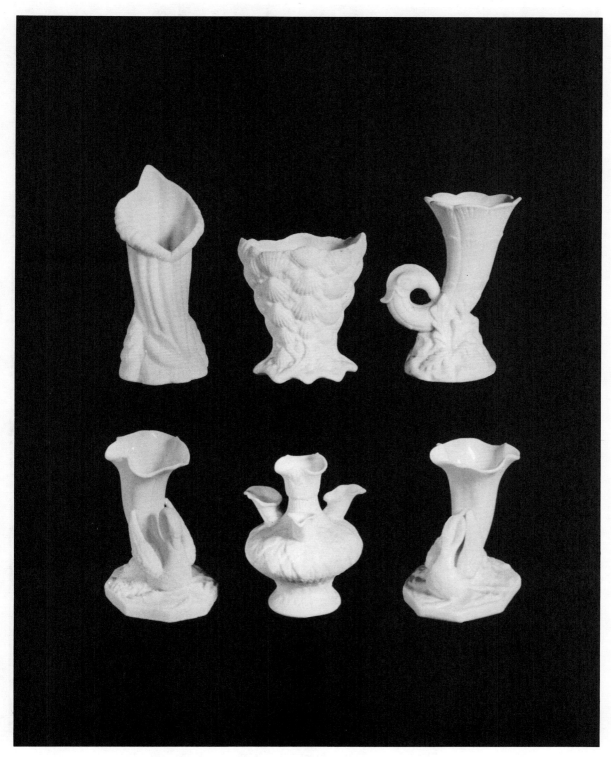

PLATE 245. PARIAN PORCELAIN VASES. 1847-1858. *Top row:* A. 6¼″ high; B. 4¼″ high; C. 5⅛″ high. *Bottom row:* D. 4½″ high; E. 4¼″ high; F. 4″ high. D. and F. appear to be a pair, but differ in height and in placement of the applied wings of the swan.

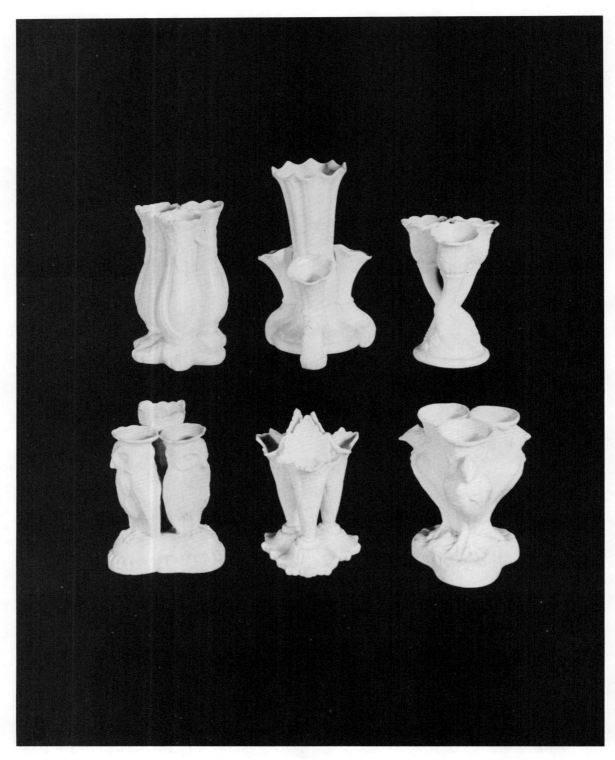

PLATE 246. Parian Porcelain Vases. 1847-1858. *Top row:* A. 5″ high; B. 6″ high; C. 4¼″ high. *Bottom row:* D. 4½″ high; E. 4¾″ high; F. 4½″ high.

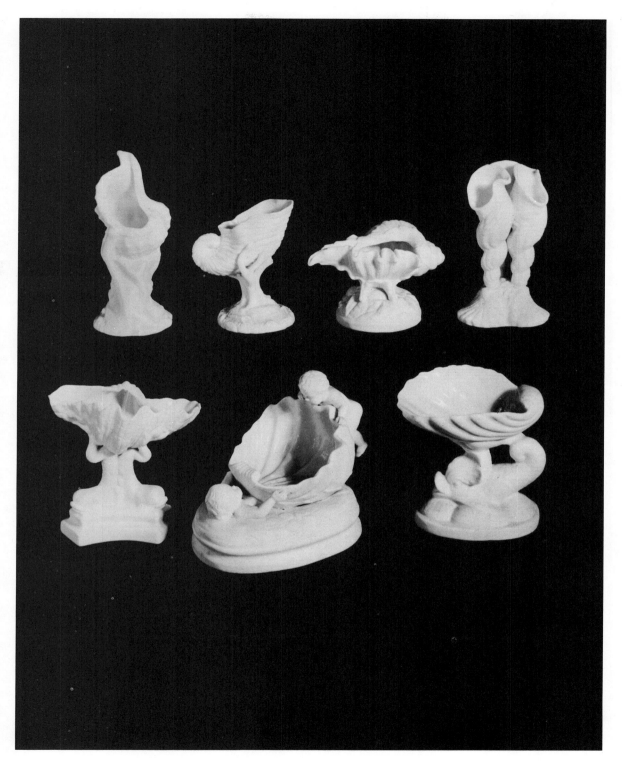

PLATE 247. Parian Porcelain Vases, Shell Motifs.
1847-1858. *Top row:* A. 5½″ high; B. 4″ high; C. 3¼″
high; D. 5″ high. *Bottom row:* E. 4½″ high; F. 5¼″
high; G. 4½″ high.

173

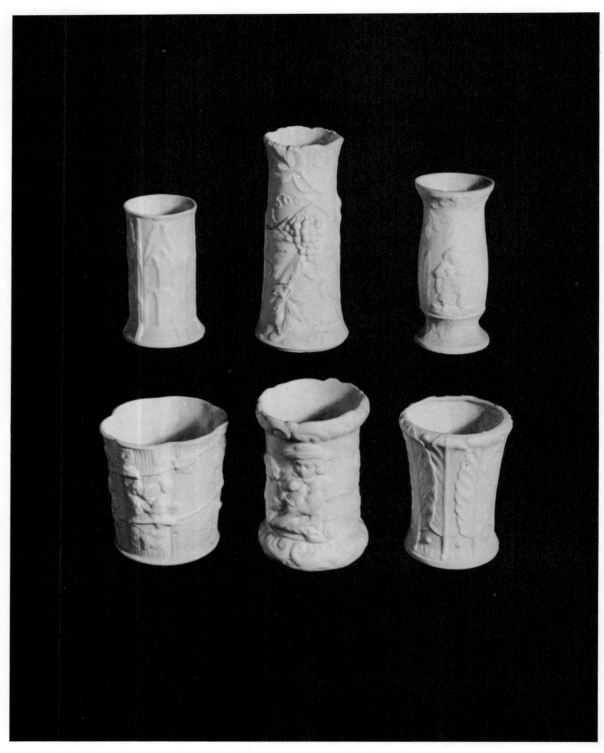

PLATE 248. PARIAN PORCELAIN VASES. 1847-1858. *Top row:* A. 4″ high; B. 6¼″ high; C. 5″ high. *Bottom row:* D. 4¾″ high; E. 4¾″ high (See also Pl. 227.) ; F. 4¼″ high.

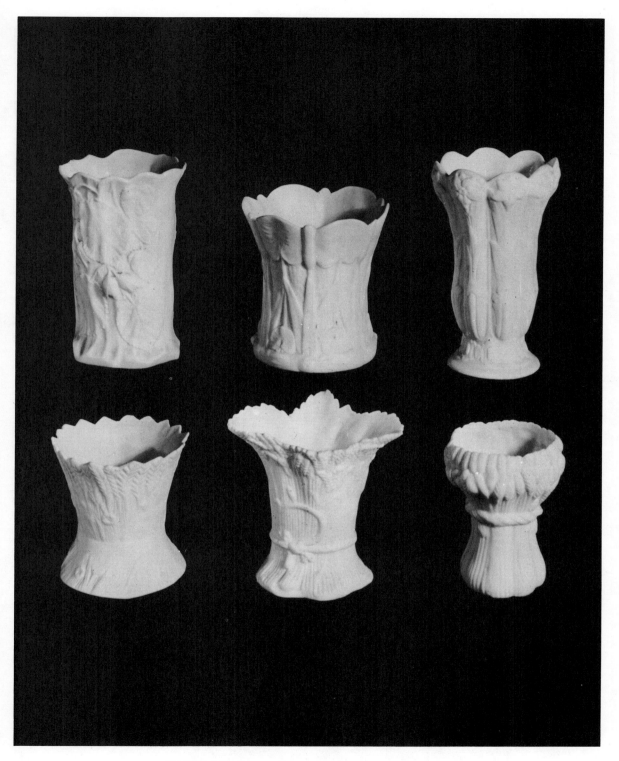

PLATE 249. Parian Porcelain Vases. 1847-1858. *Top row:* A. 5½″ high; B. 4½″ high; C. 6″ high. *Bottom row:* D. 4¼″ high; E. 5″ high; F. 4¼″ high. (See also Pl. 443G.)

PLATE 250. PARIAN PORCELAIN VASES. 1847-1858. *Top row:* A. Same as C, 4½″ high; B. 3″ high; C. Same as A. *Bottom row:* D. Same as F, 5″ high; E. 3½″ high; F. Same as D.

PLATE 251. PARIAN PORCELAIN VASES. 1847-1858. A. No applied decoration or handles, 11″ high; B. Applied grapes and handles, 10½″ high; C. Same as B, except top has been ground off, 10″ high. (See also Pls. 64, 103C, 232E, 228, 276G and 290.)

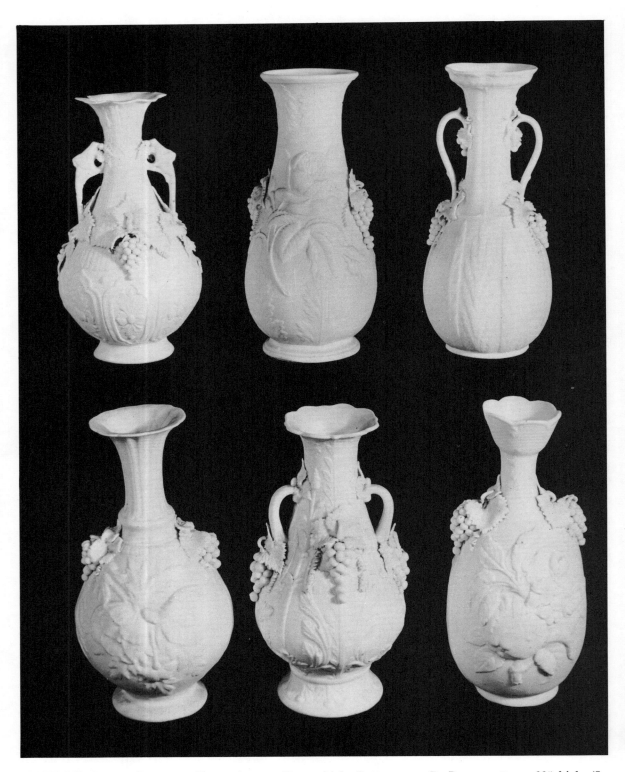

PLATE 252. Parian Porcelain Vases, Applied Decoration. 1847-1858. *Top row:* A. 10″ high (See also Pls. 264G, 264H and 285C.) ; B. 10¼″ high; C. 10¼″ high. *Bottom row:* D. Poppy pattern, 11″ high (See also Pl. 279.) ; E. 10¾″ high; F. 11″ high, (See also Pl. 274A.)

178

PLATE 253. COMPARISON PIECES, NOTE CAREFULLY.
A. Parian, grape-decorated, note especially the size of
grapes and detail in leaves, 9″ high. Compare with
B, probably made by Copeland in England, fine grapes
and leaf detail. Similar Parian grape-decorated vases
and statuettes are among the most difficult pieces to
identify positively, as no marked examples are known.

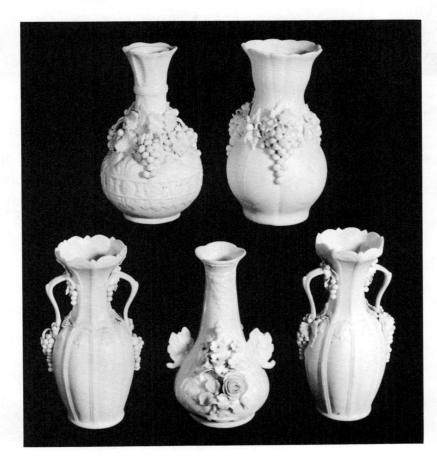

PLATE 254. PARIAN PORCELAIN VASES AND COLOGNE
BOTTLE, APPLIED DECORATION. 1847-1858. *Top row:*
A. Cologne bottle, 6″ high; B. 6″ high. *Bottom row:*
C. and E. Pair, 6⅛″ high; D. 6″ high. (See also Pl.
260E.)

PLATE 255. PARIAN PORCELAIN VASES, APPLIED DECORATION. 1847-1858. *Top row:* A. Copied from English design, 4¾″ high; B. 4⅝″ high; C. 4⅜″ high. B and C show rare restraint. *Bottom row:* D. and F. Pair, 9½″ high; E. 8½″ high.

PLATE 256. PARIAN PORCELAIN VASES, APPLIED DEC-
ORATION. 1847-1858. Four pairs. *Top row:* A. and B.
7½" high; C. and D. 7½" high. *Bottom row:* E. and F.
8½" high; G. and H. 8½" high.

PLATE 257. Parian Porcelain Vases, Applied Decoration. 1847-1858. *Top row:* A. 6¾″ high; B. 7½″ high; C. 8″ high; D. 7″ high (See also Pl. 302E.) ; E. 6¼″ high. *Bottom row:* F. 6¼″ high; G. 7½″ high; H. 7½″ high (See also Pl. 282G.) ; I. 7″ high (See also Pl. 294E.) ; J. 6½″ high.

182

PLATE 258. PARIAN PORCELAIN VASES, APPLIED DECORATION. 1847-1858. Four pairs. *Top row:* A. and B. 5⅞″ high; C. and D. 6⅞″ high. *Bottom row:* E. and F. 7¾″ high; G. and H. 7½″ high. (See also Pls. 283H and 283I.) Many of the Parian vases were also made in blue and white porcelain.

PLATE 259. PARIAN PORCELAIN VASES. 1847-1858. *Top row:* A. 6⅝″ high; B. 6¼″ high; C. 5⅝″ high; D. 4¼″ high. *Bottom row:* E. 9½″ high; F. 9¼″ high; G. 9¾″ high (See also Pl. 272D.) ; H. 9⅝″ high.

PLATE 260. PARIAN PORCELAIN VASES, APPLIED DECORATION. 1847-1858. *Top row:* A. 5″ high; B. 5¾″ high; C. 8¼″ high; D. 6″ high; E. 6″ high. (See also Pl. 254D.)

Bottom row: F. 7¼″ high; G. 8¾″ high; H. 8″ high; I. 8½″ high (See also Pls. 225A, 225B, 230B, 287B, 287H and 307J.) ; J. 7½″ high.

185

PLATE 261. PARIAN PORCELAIN VASES, APPLIED DECORATION. 1847-1858. *Top row:* A. and C. Pair, 8″ high; B. Rare design handles, 8½″ high. *Bottom row:* D. and F. Pair, 8″ high (See also Pl. 286F.) ; E. Eagle, 8″ high. (See also Pls. 280B, 280C and 280D.)

PLATE 262. PARIAN PORCELAIN VASES, APPLIED DEC-
ORATION. 1847-1858. *Top row:* A. and B. Pair, Beehive
pattern, 6¼″ high; C. and D. Pair, 7″ high. *Bottom*
row: E. 8⅞″ high; F. 9¼″ high; G. and H. Pair, 7½″
high. These patterns were strongly influenced by
English and French designs.

PLATE 263. PARIAN PORCELAIN VASES. 1847-1858. A, B and C have applied grapes, D, E and F have molded grapes. *Top row:* A. and C. Pair, 8¼″ high; B. 6½″ high. *Bottom row:* D. and F. Pair, 9″ high; E. 6¼″ high.

COLOR PLATES

COLOR PLATE A. Wares shown here were made at Bennington from 1847 to 1858. *Top row:* Cow creamer, graniteware; poodle, Rockingham; vase, blue and white porcelain, with applied handles and grape decoration; poodle, Parian; cow creamer, yellowware. *Center row:* Bottle, flint enamel; pitcher, Wild Rose pattern, with applied color; lion on base, flint enamel; "presentation" pitcher, graniteware; toby jug, scroddled ware. *Bottom row:* Pitcher, Palm Tree pattern, tan and white porcelain; Staffordshire-type cottage vase, colored decoration, gold leaf; "The Tight Shoe" statuette, Parian; pitcher, scroddled ware; "Praying Samuel" statuette, Parian; cottage vase (matches other vase); Swiss lady change cover, flint enamel.

COLOR PLATE B. Washbowl and pitcher, brilliantly colored flint enamel. Various metallic oxides—cobalt for blue, copper for green, manganese for brown—in fine powders were sprinkled onto biscuit pieces and then fired. The "Flint Enamel" process for applying powdered colors was patented by Christopher Webber Fenton in 1849.

COLOR PLATE C. Rare lamps with flint enamel bases. Such bases were made in three sizes. All or most of the glass fittings for the Bennington-made lamps were produced at the Sandwich glass factory in Massachusetts.

COLOR PLATE D. Many pitchers, as well as vases, ewers, cologne bottles and trinket boxes, were made in Parian or blue and white porcelain. *Top row:* Ewers, blue and white porcelain; vase, purple glazed grapes and green leaves, a variation of unglazed Parian. (Japanese reproductions of this vase have been made with highly glazed light blue grapes, or without additional color.) *Bottom row:* Pitchers, blue and white porcelain; trinket box, applied Parian flowers. The blue color, actually clay colored with cobalt, was painted on the inside of the mold before the piece was made, not applied to the piece itself.

COLOR PLATE E. Ewer, blue and white porcelain, made by Christopher Webber Fenton about 1853. Blue background has characteristic pinpoints, or "orange peel" surface. Excessive decoration shows superior technical craftsmanship but little regard for the original intent, which was to imitate Parian marble. Victorian insistence for decoration on almost every surface required the owner of such an ornate article to protect it by a glass dome. This design was also made in Parian porcelain without blue decoration.

COLOR PLATE F. Inkwell, finely molded gray stoneware with cobalt decoration, made about 1841. The design was inspired by one made some years earlier in England by Walley, Smith & Skinner. This inkwell was presented to John Spargo, chronicler of the history of the Bennington potteries, by the widow of Edward Norton.

COLOR PLATE G. Toby or coachman bottles by Daniel Greatbach, who came to Bennington from England. *Top row:* Dark luster or Rockingham; stoneware with cobalt decoration, only known example, marked with Fenton's 1849 mark A. *Bottom row:* Rockingham; Rockingham; flint enamel. All three are marked with Fenton's 1849 mark A.

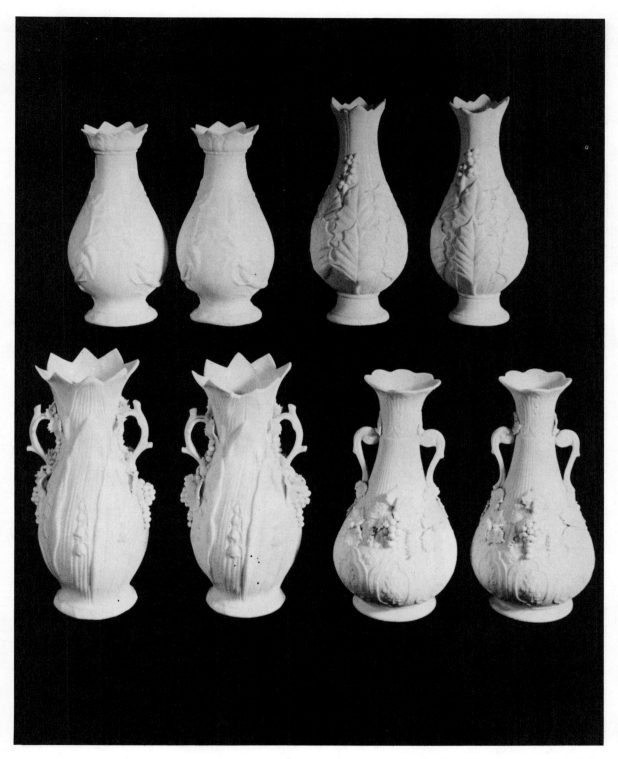

PLATE 264. PARIAN PORCELAIN VASES. 1847-1858. *Top row:* A. and B. Pair, 7¾" high; C. and D. Pair, Uncommon Holly pattern, 8½" high. *Bottom row:* E. and F. Pair, Lily of the Valley pattern, 9¾" high; G. and H. Pair, 9" high. (See also Pls. 252A and 285C.)

189

PLATE 265. PARIAN PORCELAIN VASES. 1847-1858. *Top row:* A. and B. Pair, 6¼″ high; C. and D. Pair, 6″ high. *Bottom row:* E. 8½″ high; F. 7¾″ high (Compare E and F with Pls. 278A and 293E.) ; G. 6¼″ high; H. 7½″ high.

190

PLATE 266. PARIAN PORCELAIN VASES. 1847-1858. *Top row:* A. and E. Pair, 5¼″ high; B. and D. Pair, 5¼″ high; C. 7¼″ high. *Bottom row:* F. and J. Pair, 5½″ high; G. and I. Pair, 5″ high; H. 7½″ high. (Compare G, H and I with Pl. 280, bottom row.)

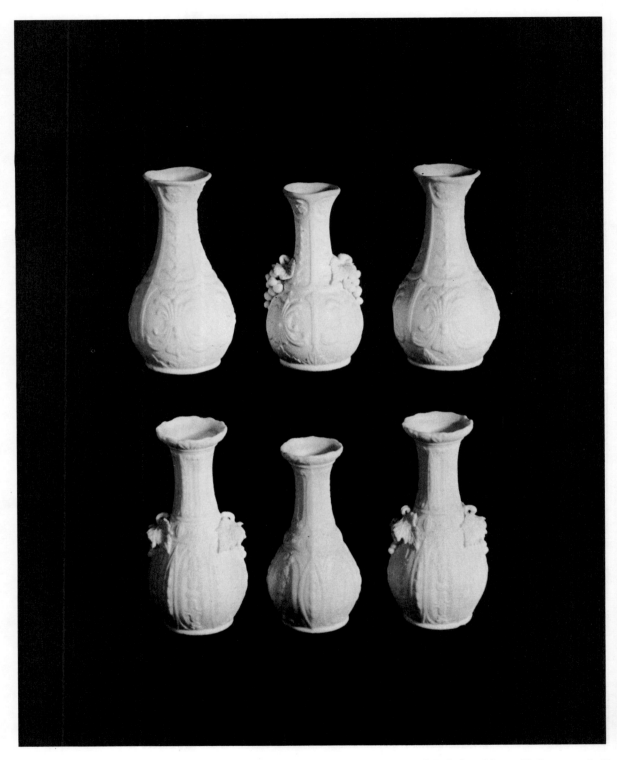

PLATE 267. Parian Porcelain Vases. 1847-1858. *Top row:* A. and C. Pair, without applied grapes, 5½″ high; B. With applied grapes, 5″ high. (See also Pl. 284A.) *Bottom row:* D. and F. Pair, with applied grapes, 5½″ high; E. Without applied grapes, 5″ high.

PLATE 268. PARIAN PORCELAIN VASES, APPLIED DEC-
ORATION. 1847-1858. *Top row:* A. 10¾″ high; B. 8½″
high; C. 6¼″ high. (Compare A, B and C with Pls. 231B, 289D, 289E, 289F, 289G and 289H.) *Bottom row:* D.
and F. Pair, 8¾″ high; E. 7½″ high (Compare D, E
and F with Pls. 288A and 288B.)

PLATE 269. PARIAN PORCELAIN VASES, APPLIED DEC-
ORATION. 1847-1858. *Top row:* A. 7¼″ high; B. 6½″
high; C. 7″ high. (Compare A, B, and C with Pls. 232D,
232F and 301D.) *Bottom row:* D. and E. Pair, 8½″
high; F. and G. Pair, 8″ high.

PLATE 270. MOLDED VASES WITH APPLIED DECORATION. 1847-1858. First five vases are Parian porcelain. *Top row:* A. 6″ high; B. 4½″ high; C. 5¼″ high. *Bottom row:* D. Same pattern as F, 7½″ high; E. Copied from design by Charles Meigh and Sons, England, 8″ high; F. Blue and white porcelain, 6½″ high.

195

PLATE 271. EXTREMELY RARE FOOTED VASES. Blue and
white porcelain, 1850-1858, 5½″ high.

PLATE 272. Blue and White Porcelain Vases. 1850-1858. *Top row:* A. and B. Duplicates, rare dark blue, 9″ high. *Bottom row:* C. and E. Pair, left and right, rare, 8½″ high; D. 9¾″ high. (See also Pl. 259G.)

PLATE 274. Blue and White Porcelain Vases. 1850-
1858. A. Extremely rare, 11¾″ high; B. Rare, 11″ high.
(See also Pls. 273, 305A and 305B.)

PLATE 273. Two Rare Porcelain Vases, Swan Handles. A. Parian, 1847-1858, 9½" high; B. Blue and
white porcelain, 1850-1858, 10½" high. (See also Pls.
274, 305A and 305B.)

PLATE 275. BLUE AND WHITE PORCELAIN AND PARIAN VASES. 1847-1858. *Top row:* A. Blue and white porcelain, same as C, 4″ high; B. Parian porcelain, 4″ high; C. Same as A. *Bottom row:* D. Blue and white por-celain, 5½″ high; E. Parian porcelain, same pattern as F, 5⅜″ high; F. Blue and white porcelain, same pattern as E, 5⅝″ high.

PLATE 276. BLUE AND WHITE PORCELAIN VASES. 1850-1858. *Top row:* A. 5⅛" high; B. 6¼" high; C. 5⅛" high. *Bottom row:* D. 4" high; E. 4" high; F. 3⅞" high; G. 3⅞" high. (See Pls. 103C, 232E, 228, 251 and 290.)

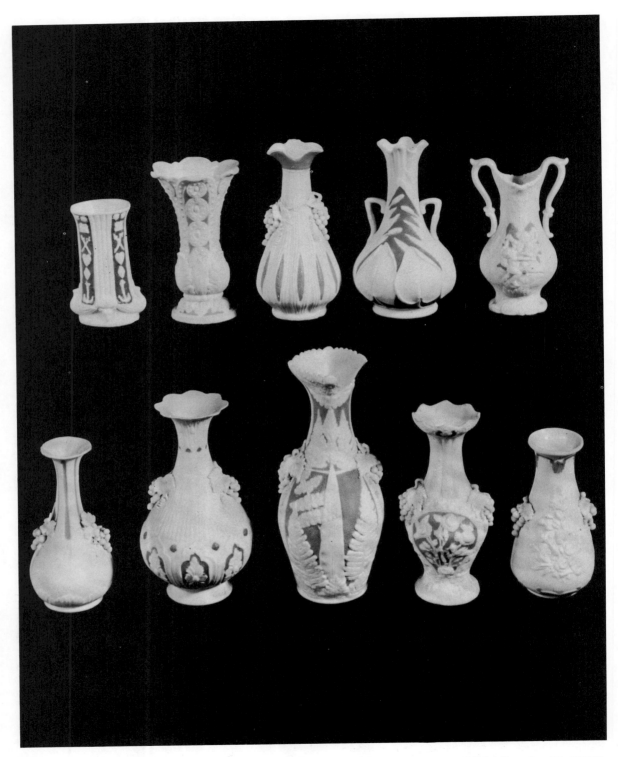

PLATE 277. BLUE AND WHITE PORCELAIN VASES. 1850-1858. *Top row:* A. 4½″ high; B. 6″ high; C. 7″ high (See also Pl. 302A.); D. 7″ high; E. 6″ high. *Bottom row:* F. 6¼″ high; G. 8″ high (See also Pl. 302C.); H. 9¾″ high (See also Pls. 275C and 275D.); I. 7¾″ high; J. 6¼″ high.

PLATE 278. BLUE AND WHITE PORCELAIN VASES. *Top row:* A. 8″ high (See also Pls. 265E, 265F and 293E.) ; B. 8¼″ high; C. 8¾″ high. *Bottom row:* D. 9¼″ high; E. 10¾″ high; F. 10¾ high.

203

PLATE 279. BLUE AND WHITE PORCELAIN VASES, POPPY PATTERN. 1850-1858. *Top row:* A. 11½" high; B. 10" high. *Bottom row:* C. 11½" high; D. 10" high; E. 8" high. (See also Pl. 252D.) This pattern was made with and without handles in blue and white and in Parian porcelain.

PLATE 280. Blue and White Porcelain Vases. 1850-1858. *Top row:* A. 10″ high (See also Pl. 226.) ; B. 8″ high; C. 7½″ high; D. 6″ high. (Compare B, C and D with Pl. 261E.) *Bottom row:* Songbird pattern. E. 4¼″ high; F. 5″ high; G. 6¼″ high; H. 8¾″ high; I. 10″ high. (Compare E, F, G, H and I with Pls. 266G, 266H and 266I.)

PLATE 281. BLUE AND WHITE PORCELAIN VASES. 1850-1858. *Top row:* A. One handle missing, 6¼″ high; B. 7″ high; C. 8″ high; D. 6¾″ high. *Bottom row:* E. 8″ high; F. 9¼″ high; G. 7¼″ high; H. 7¼″ high.

PLATE 282. BLUE AND WHITE PORCELAIN VASES. 1850-1858. *Top row:* A. 7½″ high; B. 8½″ high; C. 8⅜″ high; D. 7½″ high. *Bottom row:* E. 8½″ high; F. 10¾″ high; G. 8¾″ high (See also Pl. 257H.) ; H. 7″ high.

PLATE 283. BLUE AND WHITE PORCELAIN VASES, 1850-1858. *Top row:* A. 6″ high; B. 7″ high; C. 8″ high; D. 6¾″ high. *Bottom row:* E. 6″ high; F. 7¼″ high; G. Fewer applied grapes than E, 6″ high; H. 8¾″ high; I. 6½″ high. (See also Pls. 258G and 258H.)

PLATE 284. BLUE AND WHITE PORCELAIN VASES. 1850-1858. *Top row:* A. 5″ high (Compare with Pls. 267A, 267B and 267C.) ; B. Uncommon amount of blue, 5″ high; C. 5½″ high; D. 5¾″ high. *Bottom row:* E. 7¾″ high; F. 8¾″ high; G. 8¾″ high; H. Duplicate of Pl. 282G, 8¾″ high.

PLATE 285. Blue and White Porcelain Vases. 1850-1858. *Top row:* A. 9½″ high; B. 9″ high; C. 9¾″ high. (See also Pls. 252A, 264G and 264H.) *Bottom row:* D. 9¼″ high; E. Duplicate of Pl. 270F, 6¾″ high; F. 9¾″ high.

PLATE 286. Blue and White Porcelain Vases. 1850-1858. *Top row:* A. 8¼″ high; B. 8″ high; C. 8½″ high. *Bottom row:* D. 8″ high; E. 10½″ high; F. 8″ high. (See also Pls. 261D and 261F.)

211

PLATE 287. BLUE AND WHITE PORCELAIN VASES. 1850-1858. *Top row:* A. 7¾″ high; B. 8¼″ high (See also Pls. 225A, 225B, 230B, 260I and 307J.) ; C. 9″ high; D. 7″ high. *Bottom row:* E. 6″ high; F. 6″ high; G. 8¾″ high; H. 8½″ high (Compare with B.) ; I. 7½″ high.

PLATE 288. BLUE AND WHITE PORCELAIN VASES. 1850-1858. Top row: A. 8½″ high; B. 7¼″ high (See also Pls. 268D, 268E and 268F.) *Bottom row:* C. 6¼″ high; D. 8¼″ high (Compare C and D with 301B and 307C.); E. 10½″ high.

PLATE 289. BLUE AND WHITE PORCELAIN VASES. 1850-1858. *Top row:* A. 8″ high; B. 11″ high; C. 13″ high. *Bottom row:* D. 11″ high; E. 8″ high; F. 7″ high; G. 6″ high; H. 6″ high. (Compare D, E, F, G and H with Pls. 231B, 268A, 268B and 268C.)

214

PLATE 290. BLUE AND WHITE PORCELAIN VASES. 1850-1858. *Top row:* A. 8¾″ high; B. Broken, 9¼″ high. *Bottom row:* C. 10″ high; D. One handle missing, 12″ high; E. 9¾″ high. (Compare all of these vases with Pls. 64, 103C, 228, 232E, 251 and 276G.)

215

PLATE 291. BLUE AND WHITE PORCELAIN VASES. 1850-1858. *Top row:* A. 4½" high; B. Lily of the Valley pattern, blue base, 4½" high, rare; C. 8" high; D. Ear of Corn pattern, blue leaves, rare, 5" high (See also Pls. 236 and 237.); E. 4¼" high. *Bottom row:* F. 5" high; G. Same as 228C, 6¼" high; H. 9" high; I. 6¾" high; J. 4" high. (Compare H, I and J with Pls. 231C and 231D.)

PLATE 292. BLUE AND WHITE PORCELAIN VASES. 1850-1858. *Top row:* A. 8¼″ high; B. 7½″ high; C. 7¼″ high; D. 6¼″ high. *Bottom row:* E. Handles, 8½″ high; F. Same as E, without handles, 8½″ high; G. 7½″ high; H. 6¼″ high. (Compare E, F, G and H with Pls. 229C, 229D, 229E and 231A.)

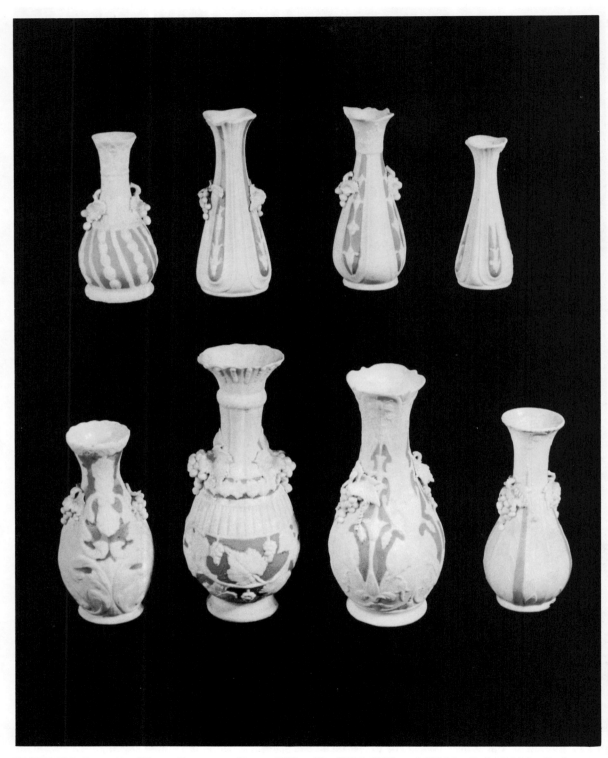

PLATE 293. BLUE AND WHITE PORCELAIN VASES. 1850-1858. *Top row:* A. 5¾″ high; B. 6¼″ high; C. 6¼″ high; D. 5¼″ high. *Bottom row:* E. 7″ high (See also Pls. 265E, 265F and 278A.) ; F. 9½″ high; G. Same as 292F, 8½″ high; H. 7″ high.

PLATE 294. Blue and White Porcelain Vases. 1850-1858. *Top row:* A. 6¼″ high; B. 9″ high; C. 8″ high; D. 6¾″ high; E. 6¾″ high. (See also Pl. 257I.) *Bottom row:* F. 8″ high; G. 8″ high; H. 7½″ high; I. 7½″ high.

PLATE 295. EXCEPTIONALLY FINE PARIAN PORCELAIN EWER. 1847-1858. A presentation piece, this is the only known example, 19″ high. Diamond shapes in bands similar to Pl. 302F.

220

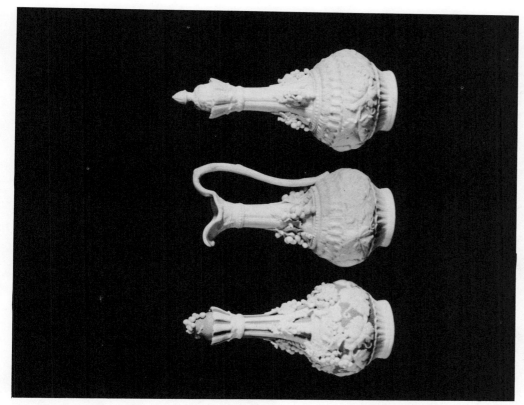

PLATE 297. Cologne Bottles and Ewer, Variations of the Same Design. 1850-1858. A. Blue and white porcelain cologne bottle, 6¾″ high without stopper; B. Parian ewer, same as Pl. 302B, 7″ high; C. Parian cologne bottle, 6¾″ high without stopper, over-all 8¼″ high.

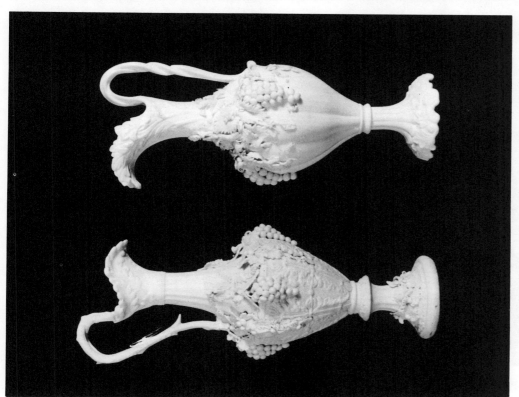

PLATE 296. Two Rare Parian Porcelain Ewers. 1847-1858. A. Extremely rare use of applied grapes on base of pedestal, 12″ high. (See also Pl. 308A.) B. Rare twisted handle, 11¼″ high.

221

PLATE 298. PARIAN PORCELAIN EWERS. 1847-1858. Three exceptionally fine examples of applied decoration. *Top row:* A. 11½″ high. *Bottom row:* B. 8¼″ high; C. 9⅛″ high.

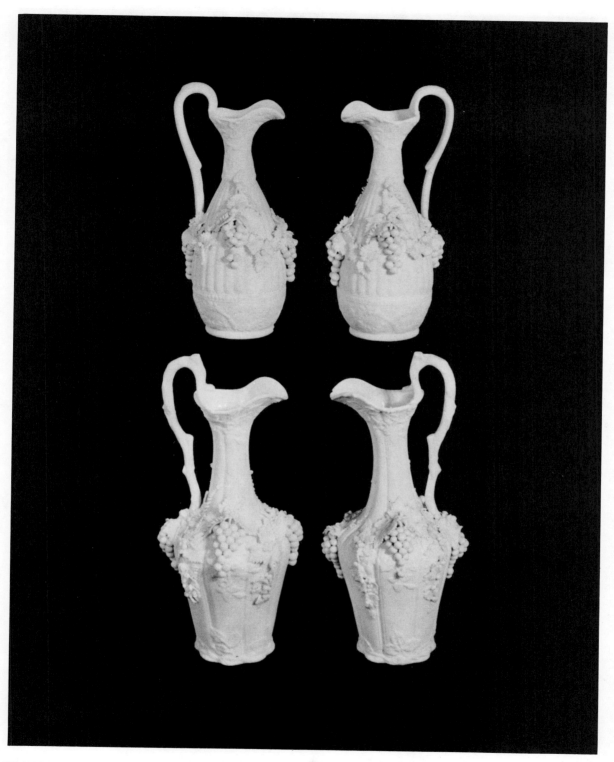

PLATE 299. Parian Porcelain Ewers. 1847-1858. *Top row:* A. and B. Reverse and obverse of pair, 8½" high. *Bottom row:* C. and D. Reverse and obverse of pair, 10½" high.

PLATE 300. PARIAN PORCELAIN EWERS. 1847-1858. Each in two sizes. *Top row:* A. 8½" high; B. 6⅞" high. *Bottom row:* C. Top not pierced, 11" high; D. Top pierced, 13" high.

224

PLATE 301. PARIAN PORCELAIN VASES AND EWER, AP-
PLIED DECORATION. 1847-1858. A. 8½″ high; B. 8½″
high (See also Pls. 288C, 288D and 307C.); C. 7¾″
high; D. 10¾″ high (See also Pls. 232D, 232F, 269A,
269B and 269C.); E. Ewer, 9½″ high.

PLATE 302. PARIAN EWERS, APPLIED DECORATION. 1847-1858. *Top row:* 7″ high (See also Pls. 277C and 307F.) ; B. 7½″ high (See also Pls. 297A, 297B and 297C.) ; C. 7¼″ high. (See also Pl. 277G.) *Bottom row:* D. 5¼″ high; E. 7″ high (See also Pl. 257D.) ; F. 7¾″ high (See also Pl. 295.) ; G. 7¼″ high; H. 6″ high.

PLATE 303. PARIAN PORCELAIN EWERS. 1847-1858. *Top row:* A. 6¾″ high; B. 8½″ high; C. 6¾″ high. *Bottom* row: D. 9″ high; E. Grapes molded, not applied, 10″ high; F. 9¼″ high.

PLATE 304. Blue and White Porcelain Ewer. 1847-1858, only known example of this graceful design, 12½" high.

PLATE 305. BLUE AND WHITE PORCELAIN EWERS. 1850-1858. Rare Morning Glory pattern, with applied grape decoration. A. 7½" high; B. 10⅞" high. (See also Pls. 273A, 273B and 274B.)

PLATE 306. Blue and White Porcelain Ewers. 1850-1858. *Top row:* A. 5¼" high; B. 9" high; C. 5¾" high. *Center row:* D. 5½" high; E. 5" high. *Bottom row:* F. 7¼" high; G. 7" high; H. 7" high.

PLATE 307. BLUE AND WHITE PORCELAIN EWERS. 1850-1858. *Top row:* A. 9¾" high. *Second row:* B. 8" high; C. 8" high. *Third row:* D. 6¾" high; E. 7¾" high; F. 7" high. (See also Pls. 277C and 302A.) *Bottom row:* G. 5¾" high; H. 7" high; I. 6¼" high; J. 6¼" high. (See also Pls. 225A, 225B, 230B, 230H, 260I and 287B.)

PLATE 308. BLUE AND WHITE PORCELAIN EWERS. 1850-1858. *Top row:* A. Extremely rare use of applied grapes on base of pedestal, 12½″ high. (See also Pl. 296A.) *Bottom row:* B. Daffodil pattern, rare, 8″ high; C. Composite design of several patterns, 8″ high.

PLATE 309. BLUE AND WHITE PORCELAIN VASES AND
EWERS. 1850-1858. *Top row:* A. 5″ high; B. 4⅞″ high.
Bottom row: C. 8″ high; D. 10″ high; E. 7½″ high.

PLATE 310. Parian Cologne Bottles, Applied Flowers. 1847-1858. Uncommon pair, with covers, 7″ high.

PLATE 311. RARE COLOGNE BOTTLES, APPLIED GRAPES
AND HANDLES. 1850-1858. A. Blue and white porcelain,
6½″ high, including cover; B. Parian, top missing,
5¾″ high.

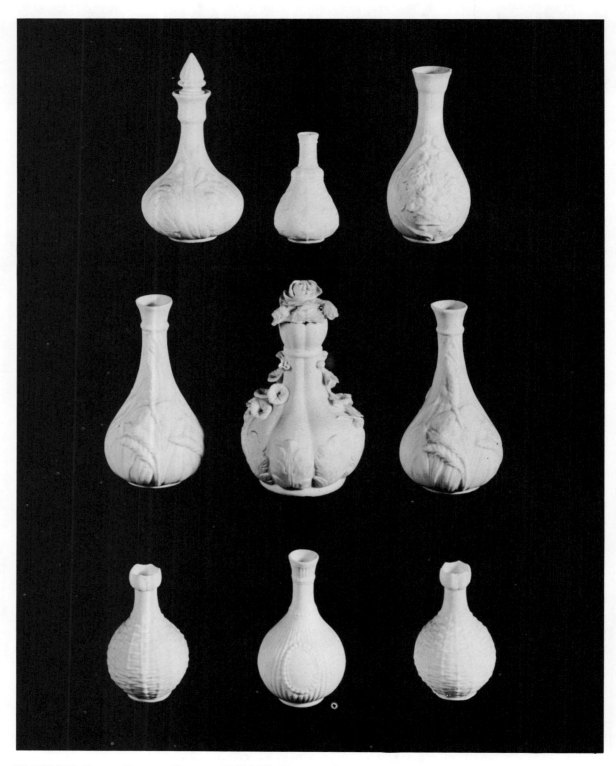

PLATE 312. PARIAN COLOGNE BOTTLES. 1847-1858. *Top row:* A. 5¼″ high; B. 3″ high; C. 4¾″ high. *Center row:* D. and F. pair, 5″ high; E. Applied flowers on sides and stopper, 5¾″ high. *Bottom row:* G. and I. Pair, 3½″ high; H. 4″ high. Matching stoppers for cologne bottles are extremely rare.

236

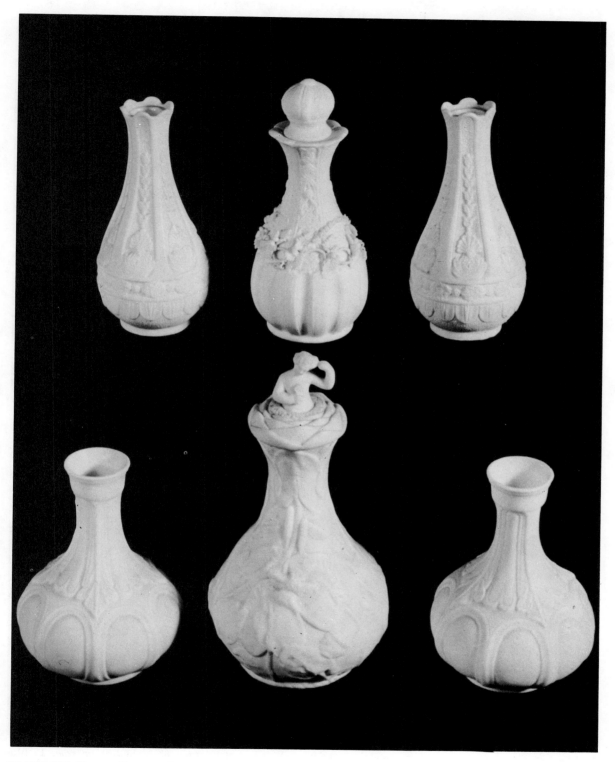

PLATE 313. PARIAN COLOGNE BOTTLES. 1847-1858. *Top row:* A. and C. Pair, 5⅞″ high; B. Same applied decoration as Pl. 318A, 6½″ high. *Bottom row:* D. and F. Pair, 5¾″ high; E. Pond Lily pattern, with blossom and figure stopper, 9″ high.

237

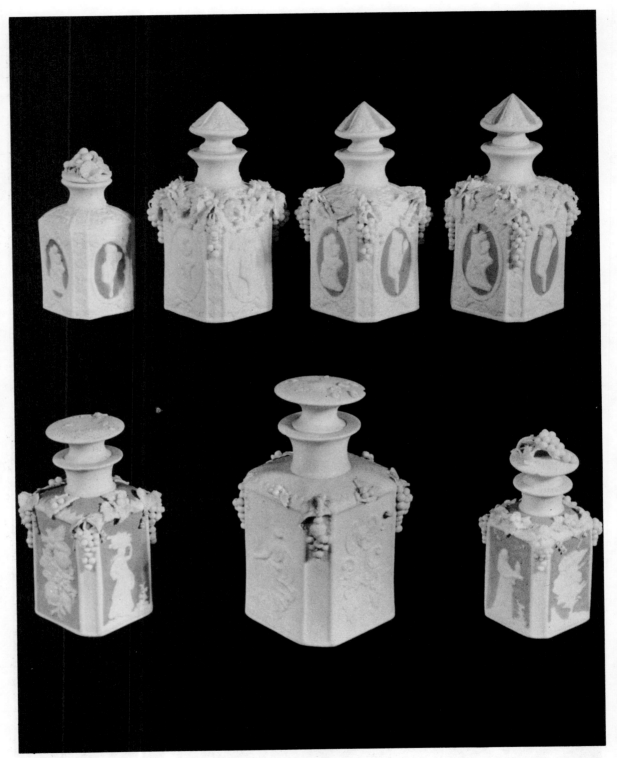

PLATE 314. Cologne Bottles, Applied Grapes. 1850-1858. A, B, C and D, same pattern. (See also Pl. 315.) *Top row:* A. Blue and white porcelain, small size, 4¾" high; B. Parian, 6" high; C. and D. Pair, blue and white porcelain, each 6" high. *Bottom row:* E. Blue and white porcelain, 5¾" high; F. Parian, 7" high; G. Blue and white porcelain, 5¾" high, including grapes on top.

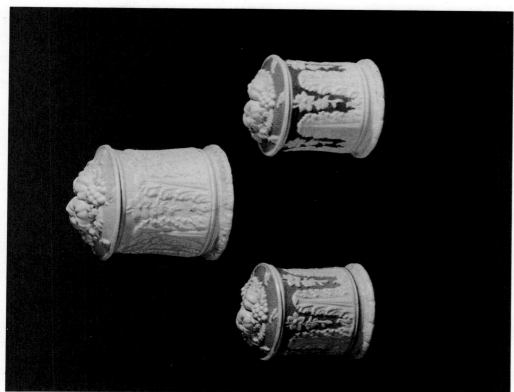

PLATE 316. THREE COVERED JARS. 1850-1858. Molded fruit on cover, Acanthus Leaf base decoration. *Top row:* A. Parian, 6¼" high x 5" diam. *Bottom row:* B. Only known example in salmon pink and blue, with gold stripes, 4¾" high x 3¾" diam.; C. Blue and white porcelain, 4¾" high x 3¾" diam.

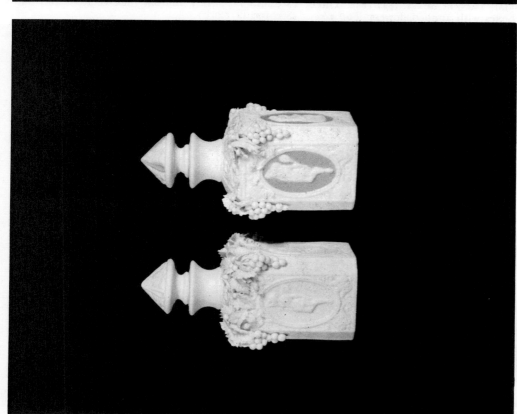

PLATE 315. COLOGNE BOTTLES, APPLIED DECORATION. 1850-1858. A. Parian, 6" high; B. Blue and white porcelain, 6" high (See also Pls. 314A, 314B, 314C and 314D.)

239

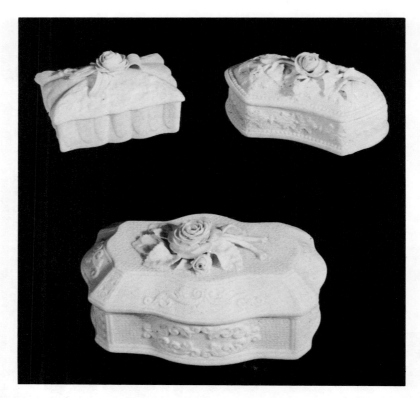

PLATE 317. Parian Trinket Boxes. 1847-1858. Three extremely rare boxes with applied flowers. *Top row:* A. Rosebud (See also Pl. 321D.) ; B. Curved, rosebud. (See also Pl. 324E.) *Bottom row:* C. Rose and bud. (See also Pl. 320J.)

PLATE 318. Blue and White Porcelain Covered Jars. 1850-1858. A. Only known example of footed bowl with elaborate applied grape decoration, 5″ high; B. Extremely rare size, 4½″ high. (See also Pl. 319B.)

PLATE 319. COVERED JARS, PORCELAIN. 1847-1858. *Top row:* A. Blue and white, molded grapes, 4″ high x 5″ diam.; B. Blue and white, 3¾″ high x 4¼″ diam. *Bottom row:* C. Blue and white, without grapes, 4″ high x 4¼″ diam.; D. Parian, applied grapes, 4¾″ high x 4¼″ diam.; E. Blue and white, applied grapes, 4½″ high x 4¼″ diam.

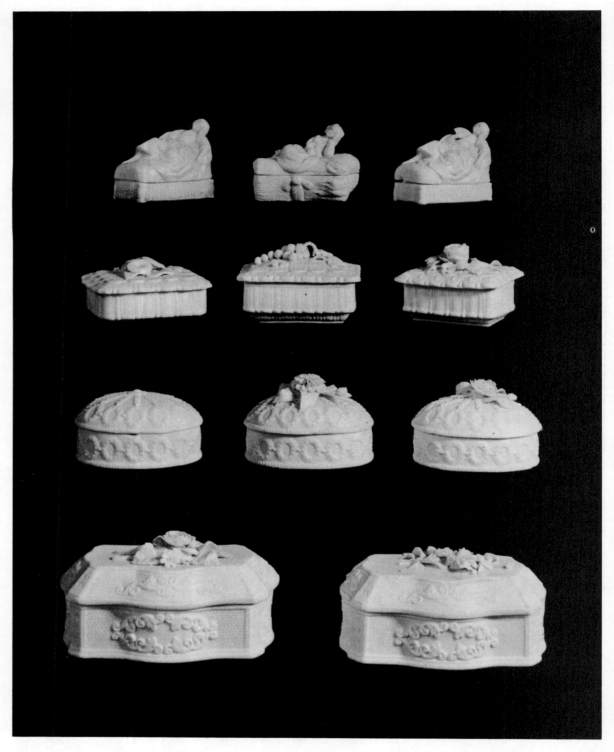

PLATE 320. PARIAN TRINKET BOXES. 1847-1858. *Top row:* A. Reclining girl on couch, without fan; B. Reclining girl on sheaf of wheat; C. Reclining girl on couch, with fan. *Second row:* D. Ribbed, morning glories; E. Ribbed, with grapes; F. Ribbed, rose. *Third row:* G. Ovals, plain top; H. Ovals, flower top; I. Ovals, rose top. (Compare G, H and I with Pls. 328D and 328E.) *Bottom row:* J. and K. (See also Pl. 317C.)

242

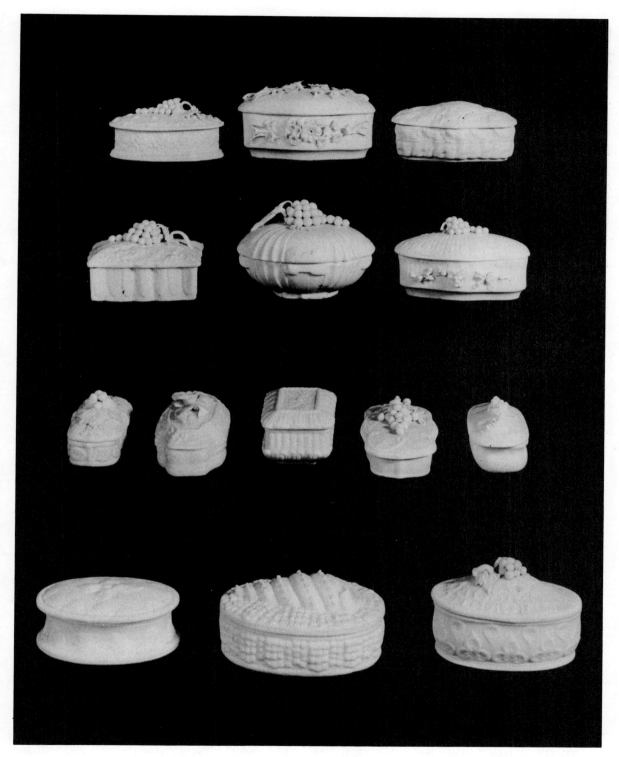

PLATE 321. PARIAN TRINKET BOXES. 1847-1858. *Top row:* A. Conventional leaf pattern, grape top; B. Applied flowers in plain rectangular box; C. Vine on ribs, plain top. *Second row:* D. Grape top (See also Pl. 317A.); E. Round, ribbed, grape top; F. Applied grapes on sides and top. *Third row:* G. Grape top; H. Flower top; I. Molded flower design top; J. Grape top; K. Grape top. *Bottom row:* L. Conventional leaves and flower top; M. Seashell top, with glazed polka-dots; N. Conventionalized design, grape top.

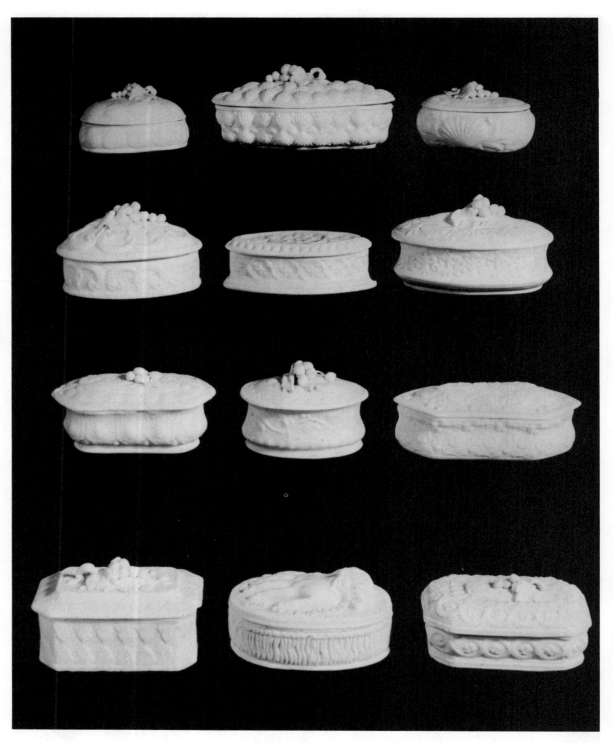

PLATE 322. PARIAN TRINKET BOXES. 1847-1858. *Top row:* A. Grape top (See also Pl. 331G.) ; B. Shells (See also Pl. 326B.) ; C. Shell with grapes (See also Pl. 329D.) *Second row:* D. Scrolls (See also Pls. 331B and 331E.) ; E. Oriental design (See also Pls. 329B and 331F.) ; F. Conventional leaf. (See also Pl. 326L.)

Third row: G. Oval and ribs (See also Pls. 328B and 328C.) ; H. Round, with vine (See also Pl. 326C.) ; I. All-over roses, no grapes. *Bottom row:* J. Pointed leaf band (See also Pl. 331L.) ; K. Hand on top; L. Circles with flowers. (See also Pl. 331H.)

244

PLATE 323. PARIAN TRINKET BOXES. 1847-1858. *Top row:* A. Plain top; B. Grape top. *Second row:* C. Masks on corners, grape top; D. Masks on corners, plain top; E. Molded greyhound on top. (See also Pl. 327E.) *Third row:* F. Molded flowers on top, wheat on sides; G. Cherub with lamb; H. Molded classic figure on top and sides. *Bottom row:* I. Diamond shape; J. Diamond shape, applied roses; K. Blue and white porcelain on top only.

245

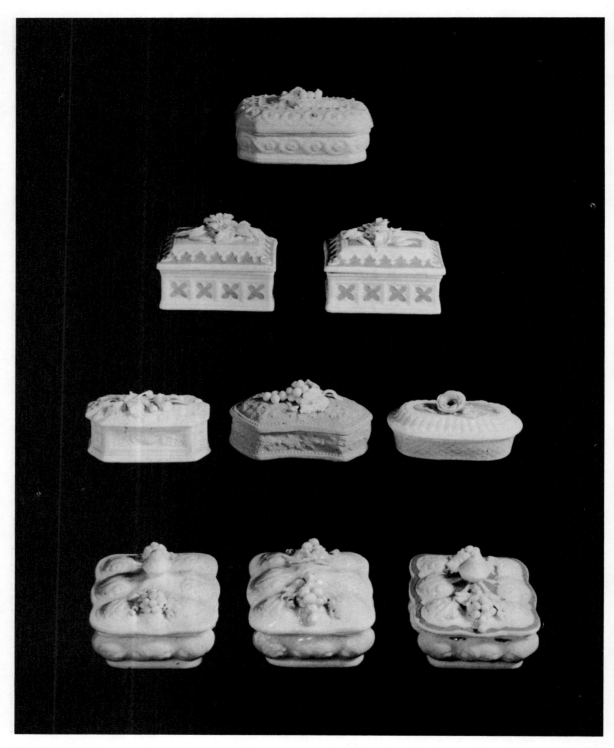

PLATE 324. TRINKET BOXES, ASSORTED MATERIALS. 1847-1858. *Top row:* A. Parian, flowers in circles, same as Pl. 322L. *Second row:* B. and C. Blue and white porcelain, Gothic circles on top, quatrefoil design on sides, assorted applied flowers on top. *Third row:* D. Parian, applied flowers on top; E. Extremely rare so-called "Harrison Blue" porcelain, curved box (See also Pl. 433B.) ; F. Parian, basket shape, applied flowers. *Bottom row:* G. Parian, pointed finial; H. Belleek, same design as G, extremely rare material (See also Pls. 225 and 401A.) ; I. Blue and white porcelain, same design as G and H.

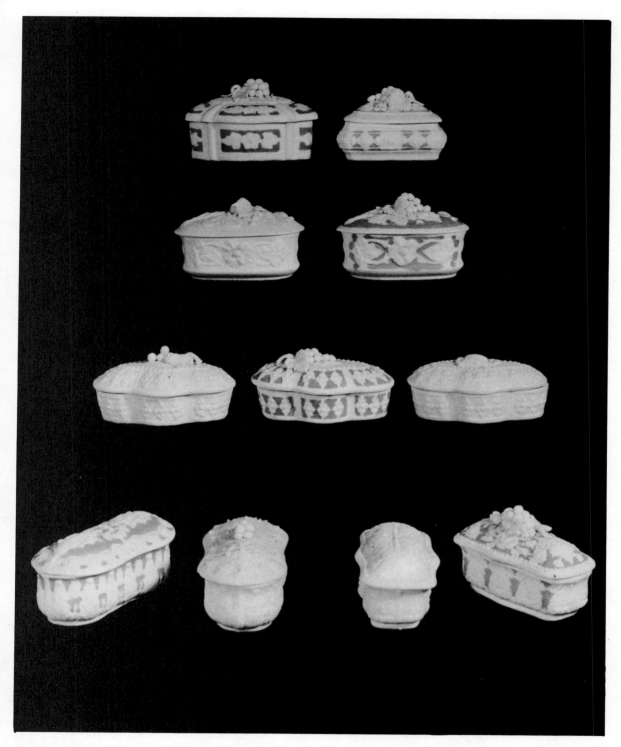

PLATE 325. PARIAN AND BLUE AND WHITE PORCELAIN TRINKET BOXES. 1847-1858. *Top row:* A. Blue and white porcelain, flower and leaf (For model for this box, see Fig. XII.) ; B. Blue and white porcelain, grape top. *Second row:* C. Parian (See also D.) ; D. Blue and white porcelain. *Third row:* Same design. E. Parian, grapes; F. Blue and white porcelain, grapes; G. Parian, molded fruit on top. *Bottom row:* H. and I. Same pattern. H. Blue and white porcelain, without grapes; I. Parian, with grapes; J. and K, same pattern; J. Parian, without grapes; K. Blue and white porcelain, with grapes.

PLATE 326. Blue and White Porcelain Trinket Boxes. 1850-1858. *Top row:* A. Alternate colored ribs; B. Shells (See also Pl. 322B.); C. Round with vine. (See also Pl. 322F.) *Second row:* D. Shell-shaped, gold polka dots (See also F.) ; E. Colored diamonds, with grapes; F. Shell-shaped. (See also D.) *Third row:* G. Conventional leaf, with grapes; D. Ducks on top, fern pattern; I. Grape top. *Bottom row:* J. Ivy leaf, grape top; K. Elliptical shape, grape top; L. Conventional leaf (See also Pl. 322F.)

PLATE 327. BLUE AND WHITE PORCELAIN TRINKET BOXES. 1850-1858. *Top row:* A. Shell (See also Pls. 322C and 329D.); B. Grape top; C. Daffodil buds. *Second row:* D. Oriental pattern (See also F.); E. Molded greyhound on top (See also Pl. 323E.); F. Oriental pattern. (See also D.) *Third row:* G. Leaf edged in blue; H. Applied flowers on top and sides; I. Conventional flowers. *Bottom row:* J. Molded classic figure on top and sides; K, L and M. Three treatments of same figure on top; N. Mask ends, grape top.

PLATE 328. BLUE AND WHITE PORCELAIN TRINKET BOXES. 1850-1858. *Top row:* A. Ovals, grape top. *Second row:* B. and C. Oval and ribs, variants. (See also Pl. 322G.) *Third row:* D. Ovals with bars (Compare with E, see also Pls. 320G, 320H and 320I.) ; E. Ovals, with-out bars (See also Pls. 320G, 320H and 320I.) *Bottom row:* F, G, H and I, same pattern. F. Parian; G. Blue and white porcelain; H. Extremely rare brown and white porcelain; I. Blue center under grapes.

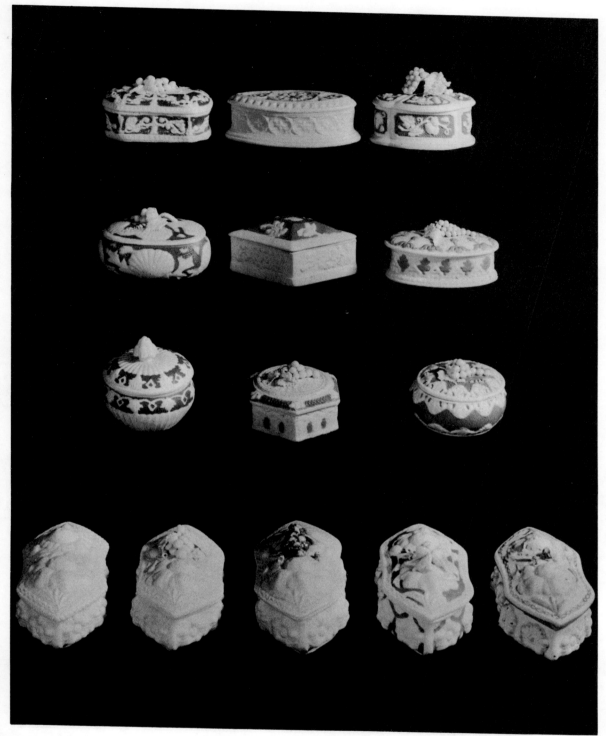

PLATE 329. Blue and White Porcelain Trinket Boxes. 1850-1858. *Top row:* A. Conventional design, grape top; B. Oriental pattern (See also Pls. 322E and 331F.) ; C. High arched grapes on top. *Second row:* D. Shell (See also Pls. 322C and 327A.) ; E. Diamond shape, same as Pl. 323K; F. Conventional design, grape top. *Third row:* G. Round, leaf and rib; H. Hexagonal shape, grape top; I. Round, grape top. *Bottom row:* J, K, L, M and N, same molded flowers pattern. J. Parian, without grapes; K. Parian, with grapes; L. Parian, gold-glazed grapes; M. Blue and white porcelain, with grapes; N. Pastel colors, grapes.

PLATE 330. TRINKET BOXES WITH CHERUBS ON TOP. 1847-1858. *Top row:* A. Blue and white porcelain, watch holder (See also Pls. 317C, 320, and 320K.) *Second row:* B. Parian (See also C.) ; C. Parian, with gold-glazed polka dots. *Third row:* D. Parian (See also E.) ; F. Blue and white porcelain (See also D.) ; F. Parian (See also G.) *Bottom row:* G. Blue and white porcelain (See also F.) ; H. Extremely fine, molded fruit in basket; I. Rare use of applied flowers in basket.

PLATE 331. BLUE AND WHITE PORCELAIN TRINKET BOXES. 1850-1858. *Top row:* A. Conventionalized design, grape top (See also Pl. 321N.) ; B. Draped figure on top, scrolls (See also E and Pl. 322D.) ; C. Ivy leaf, grape top. *Second row:* D. All-over geometric design; E. Rare dark blue (See also B and Pl. 322D.); F. Oriental design. (See also Pls. 322E and 329B.) *Third row:* G. Shells (See also Pl. 322A.); H. Circles with flowers (See also Pl. 322L.); I. Hair container, open top. *Bottom row:* J. Round, molded leaves; K. Heart-shaped box, grape top; L. Pointed leaf band. (See also Pl. 322J.)

PLATE 332. TRINKET BOXES WITH ANIMALS ON TOP. 1850-1858. All are Parian except G. *Top row:* A. Lamb on Bible, with cross; B. Partridge on diamond-shape box; C. Lamb on Bible, without cross. *Center row:* D. Dog, raised head; E. Sitting duck; F. Sleeping spaniel. *Bottom row:* G. Blue and white porcelain, lamb on diamond-shaped box; H. Bird on nest; I. Lamb on oval box.

254

PLATE 333. BLUE AND WHITE PORCELAIN TRINKET BOX.
1850-1858. Extremely rare, 5¾″ high. Only known example of a Parian cow on a trinket box.

CHAPTER FIVE: STATUETTES AND FIGURES

Statuettes were the first items to be produced at Bennington in Parian porcelain through the influence of Christopher Webber Fenton. It was soon used for many other items, although its original purpose had been to reproduce statuary items usually made in marble by costlier sculpture. Parian porcelain statuettes were made in a great variety of designs by almost every sizable pottery in England and France and by several firms in America. As late as 1878 H. F. Libby in Boston was still producing such figures in designs which were greatly influenced by the earlier Fenton items.

Even in Bennington, peddlers carried foreign Parian statuettes from door to door, so that a piece could have a local association without having been made in the town. Parian statuettes were extremely popular decorative items, and in Fenton's price list of 1852 he listed ten different figures, only some of which have been positively identified. Identification of many possibly authentic pieces is difficult, since Fenton often copied English examples almost line for line. He even favored using in his designs the traditional English dress frequently associated with Staffordshire models, so costume is not always a reliable guide in determining whether America or England was the country of origin.

This is the most difficult single group of items to identify with accuracy as Bennington-made. Much care has been taken, in assembling these examples, to include only those items which have an unimpeachable Bennington history, although future years will undoubtedly bring additions. With the exception of the Red Riding Hood figure, none of the statuettes was marked. Only two statuettes are known to have been made in materials other than Parian porcelain. The Red Riding Hood figure made in Rockingham differs slightly from the statuettes of the same motif made in Parian, but the boy with dog made in flint enamel has no known counterpart in any other ware.

PLATE 334. RARE PARIAN STATUETTE. 1847-1858. "Simply to Thy Cross I Cling" incised on cross, 13" high.

PLATE 335. EXTREMELY RARE PARIAN BUST. 1847-1858.
Flora, with necklace and headdress of applied flowers,
8⅞" high.

PLATE 336. PARIAN BUSTS. 1847-1858. Similar busts were made in England, usually a little larger than these. Busts are among the most difficult items to identify positively. These eight are among the few known to have been made in Bennington. *Top row:* A. Boy, 5″ high; B. Girl, 4¾″ high; C. Girl with bird, 5″ high; D. Apollo, 5¼″ high; E. Young girl, 5″ high. *Bottom row:* F. Milton, 5″ high; G. Byron, 5¼″ high; H. Dickens, 5″ high.

PLATE 337. RARE PARIAN STATUETTE. 1847-1858. "Autumn" design, classically draped figure holding overflowing basket of applied grapes and leaves, 13" high.

PLATE 338. RARE PARIAN STATUETTE. 1847-1858. Seated girl, with basket of applied flowers, and an applied rose and buds on headdress, very fine, 13" high.

PLATE 339. PARIAN STATUETTES. 1847-1858. *Top row:* A. "Greek Slave" from original statue of same title by Vermont sculptor Hiram Powers, 10″ high. This design was made also by Copeland. *Bottom row:* B. Classic figure with applied sword and crown at foot, "Egypt, Romans, Greece" (sic) incised on tablet, 8¾″ high; C. Girl with applied flower wreath and headdress, 9″ high.

PLATE 340. PARIAN STATUETTE. 1847-1858. Girl with bird in nest, applied bird, 8″ high.

PLATE 341. RARE PARIAN STATUETTE. 1847-1858. Boy in tricorne hat leaning on sheaf of wheat (spill holder), 10¾″ high. There should be a feminine counterpart to this design.

PLATE 342. PARIAN STATUETTES. 1847-1858. *Top row:* A. Boy with bird, 10″ high. *Bottom row:* B. and C. are a pair. B. Girl with dog, glazed polka dots, 8¾″ high. This was also made without the glazed polka dots, as in C; C. Boy with dog, also made with glazed polka dots, 9″ high.

PLATE 343. PAIR OF RARE PARIAN STATUETTES. 1847-
1858. A. Boy with basket of applied grapes, 12¼″ high;
B. Girl, with hat hanging in back, applied flowers, 12″
high. Both of these statuettes are exceptionally fine in
execution.

PLATE 344. PAIR OF PARIAN STATUETTES. 1847-1858.
A. Boy, and B. Girl with book. No applied decoration,
10" high.

PLATE 345. PARIAN ANGEL. 1847-1858. Made to be suspended from above, 6¼″ long.

PLATE 346. PARIAN STATUETTE. 1847-1858. Bacchus design, no applied decoration, molded grapes, 8″ high.

PLATE 347. RARE PARIAN STATUETTE. 1847-1858.
Cherub with basket and headdress of applied flowers,
5½" high.

PLATE 348. THREE RARE STATUETTES. 1847-1858. *Top row:* A. Parian, child reading book in chair, gold glazed polka dots, 6¼" high. *Bottom row:* B. Blue and white porcelain, girl with bird on shoulder in chair, 6½" high; C. Parian, girl with cat in chair, 7" high.

PLATE 349. PARIAN STATUETTES. 1847-1858. *Top row:* A. Praying child, 2¾" high; B. Praying child, same as Pl. 230C, 3¾" high; C. Praying girl, pair with Pl. 362A, 2¾" high. (See also Pl. 361E.) *Bottom row:* D. Sleeping child, gold trim, 3⅝" high; E. Praying angel, gold trim, 4¾" high; F. Sleeping boy, gold trim, 4" high.

PLATE 350. PARIAN STATUETTES. 1847-1858. *Top row:* A, B and C, Baby on couch. A. With applied grapes, 3⅜" high, 4¾" long; B. Holding cat, 3¼" high, 4" long; C. With applied lace, 3" high, 4¼" long. *Bottom row:* D. Two babies in hooded cradle, extremely rare, 4¾" high, 8" long; E. Kneeling child with rabbit, gold glazed polka dots, 5¼" high; F. Baby in hooded cradle, pastel color fired on hair and baby's features, 4" high, 6" long.

269

PLATE 351. PARIAN STATUETTES. 1847-1858. *Top row:* A. Classic figure, 4¾″ high; B. Begging dog spill-holder, 5″ high; C. Old man spill-holder, 4½″ high. *Bottom row:* D. Monkey with dog, 4″ high; E. Goat, smear-glazed, 3″ high; F. Sitting boy, very fine, 5″ high.

PLATE 352. PARIAN STATUETTES. 1847-1858. *Top row:* A. Man with faggots, 7½" high; B. Hunter with gun spill-holder, 6½" high; C. Fisherman with basket, 7¼" high. *Bottom row:* D. Boy with basket of applied eggs, 9¾" high; E. Milton, 9" high; F. Frowning girl with applied marbles, 9½" high.

PLATE 353. Parian Statuettes. 1847-1858. *Top row:* A. Child with laurel wreath on head, spill-holder, 6½" high. *Bottom row:* B. and C. pair, B. Child on left, spill-holder, 5½" high; C. Child on right, spill-holder, 5¾" high.

PLATE 354. Parian Statuettes and Two Whistles. 1847-1858. *Top row:* A. Red Riding Hood, 3¼" high; B. Eagle and baby, rare as an inkwell, 5" high (See also Pl. 399B) ; C. Pig, 1½" high, 2½" long. *Bottom row:* D. Swan whistle in graniteware, 2¼" high, 2½" long; E. Baby resting on basket, 3¾" high; F. Whistle, 3" long.

PLATE 355. TWO EXTREMELY RARE STATUETTES. 1849-
1858. A. Flint enamel statuette of boy with dog, 4¼″
high; B. Red Riding Hood in Rockingham, 3″ high.
These are the only two known statuette designs made
in flint enamel and Rockingham.

PLATE 356. PARIAN STATUETTES. 1847-1858. *Top row:* A, B and C, "The Tight Shoe." A. Rare type, 3½" high; B. 4¾" high; C. 3¾" high. *Bottom row:* D. Red Riding Hood, 1847-1848, same as F, except marked with Fenton's Works mark E, rare with mark, 6⅜" high; E. 3¼" high; F. Same as D, except unmarked, 6⅜" high.

PLATE 358. PARIAN STATUETTES. 1847-1858. A. Praying girl with book on left knee, 8½" high; B. Same girl, ribbed base, 9" high.

PLATE 357. PARIAN STATUETTES. 1847-1858. A. Praying girl with book on left knee, 8½" high (Compare girl with Pl. 358A, base with Pl. 358B. See also Pl. 359A, girl with book on right knee.) ; B. Girl with lyre, 8¼" high (Compare base with Pl. 359C.)

PLATE 359. PARIAN STATUETTES. 1847-1858. *Top row:* A. Praying girl with book on right knee, 8½″ high (See also Pls. 357A, 358A and 358B.) *Bottom row: B.* Girl with harp, 8¼″ high; C. Girl with lyre, ribbed base, 8½″ high (See also Pl. 357B.)

PLATE 360. GRANITEWARE STATUETTE. 1850-1858. Only known example of this size in this material, 13¼″ high.

PLATE 361. PARIAN STATUETTES. 1847-1858. *Top row:* A. 5″ high, same as Pl. 362D; B. Praying child, 6″ high. *Bottom row:* C. Same as Pl. 349B; D. Praying child, cushion decorated with gold, extremely rare large size, 13″ high; E. Same as Pl. 349C, except smaller size, 2¾″ high.

PLATE 362. PARIAN STATUETTES. 1847-1858. *Top row:* A. Praying girl, pair with Pl. 349C, 2¾″ high; B. Praying child, 3¼″ high; C. Praying child, 2½″ high. *Bottom row:* D. Praying Samuel, smear-glazed, 4¾″ high; E. Praying Samuel, 3½″ high; F. Praying Samuel, 4¾″ high. This design was also made in England, but is usually marked. Small Parian statuettes of praying children were popular and were made in quantity at many different potteries.

279

CHAPTER SIX: ANIMALS AND BIRDS

The deer, lion and poodle figures are today among the most sought-after of all the Bennington-made ceramic items. As in the case of the decorative statuettes, the collector should exercise caution in accepting animal or bird figures as Bennington-made if they are not included as illustrated examples here.

Never produced in great quantity, the animal figures were made for mantel decoration in pairs. Does and stags faced each other and right- and left-facing poodles and lions were made in all combinations. The extremely rare recumbent cows were also made in pairs, but for some reason no bulls are known to have been made as companion pieces.

The deer and poodles were made in Rockingham and flint enamel and rarely in Parian, although no known example of a Bennington lion or cow has yet been found in Parian. There is no reason to believe, however, that they were not made in this material, and lucky will be the collector who possesses either a Parian lion or cow. On the other hand, none of the other animals or birds (except the cow creamers) was ever made in any material but Parian. So the field of discovery is open to everyone.

No sitting poodles were ever made at Bennington. Such examples in Rockingham ware, made in East Liverpool, Ohio, are frequently offered as Bennington products. The famous Bennington poodles were always erect and each holds a basket in its mouth. An occasional example of a poodle without the basket may be found, but careful examination will usually reveal that the basket was either broken off or intentionally removed before glazing. Sitting or reclining dogs on cushions were made as small ornamental pieces in Parian. Some of them were designed to be used as paperweights, but these should not be confused with the traditional poodle figures.

In identifying cow creamers, it is important to note that the particular characteristics of Bennington cow creamers are also present in some English examples. At the cornerstone-laying at the Bennington Battle Monument ceremony, an enterprising Bennington dealer ordered about 300 cow creamers made up by a Staffordshire pottery from a Bennington design, to be sold as souvenirs. The sale was so successful that at the dedication cermony for the monument in 1891, the dealer was able to sell an additional 500 of the same design. The difference between the English-made cow creamers and the Bennington-made ones is in the glaze. The English ones were dipped in a solid brown glaze and lack the mottled appearance common to Bennington-made Rockingham and flint enamel. The cow creamer design was also made at Bennington in graniteware, common yellow and scroddled ware.

The marking of the Bennington animal figures seems to have been limited to the Fenton 1849 mark A, which appears only on the recumbent deer, the cows, the lions on bases and the poodle paperweights (included in Chapter Seven.) For some reason the popular cow creamers were never marked, although the base offers an excellent place. The other animal and bird forms were generally not marked, even the distinctive stoneware greyhound inkstand (included in Chapter Seven) made by the Norton Pottery.

PLATE 363. PARIAN STATUETTE OF A EWE. 1847-1858, extremely rare standing ewe, coleslaw wool, 3″ high.

PLATE 364. FLINT ENAMEL STAG. 1849-1858. Marked with 1849 mark A. Extremely rare example without tree stump spill-holder, applied coleslaw on forelock and on grass, rare use of applied flowers in grass, 10″ high to antlers, base 10¾″ long.

282

PLATE 365. FLINT ENAMEL STAG. 1849-1858. (See also Pls. 364 and 366.)

PLATE 366. Two Pairs of Recumbent Deer. 1849-1858. *Top row:* A and B. Only known examples of deer in Parian ware, both stag and doe marked with 1849 mark A, gray-black eyes. Stag 10½" high to antlers; base, 10¾" long. Doe, 8½" high to ear; base, 11" long.

Bottom row: C. Flint enamel doe, marked with 1849 mark A, 9" high to ear, base 11" long; D. Flint enamel stag, marked with 1849 mark A, 10" high to antlers, base 10¾" long.

PLATE 367. A KENNEL OF POODLES. 1849-1858. These fourteen poodles illustrate the wide variety of details, glazes and materials used. This standing poodle, with a basket in his mouth, was the only individual dog design made at Bennington.

PLATE 368. PAIR OF ROCKINGHAM POODLES. 1849-1858.
Without mustache or top-knot, rare size, 8″ high.

PLATE 369. PAIR OF FLINT ENAMEL POODLES. 1849-1858.
Without mustache or top-knot, 9″ high.

PLATE 370. EXTREMELY RARE PAIR OF GLAZED YELLOW-
WARE POODLES. 1850-1858. Only known pair of poodles
in this material, 8½″ high, 9″ long.

PLATE 371. RARE PARIAN POODLE. 1850-1858. Facing right, mustache and top-knot, 8¾″ high, 8½″ long.

288

PLATE 372. RARE PARIAN POODLE. 1850-1858. Facing
left, no mustache, with top-knot, 9¼″ high, 9″ long.

PLATE 373. EXTREMELY RARE GRANITEWARE POODLE. 1850-1858. Facing right, only known example with cobalt blue eyes, mustache and top-knot, 9½" high, 9" long.

290

PLATE 374. EXTREMELY RARE PAIR OF GRANITEWARE POODLES. 1850-1858. Made and owned by Decius Clark, C. W. Fenton's superintendent. Molded mustaches, coleslaw on hind legs, 8¼" high.

PLATE 375. EXTREMELY RARE LIGHT GREEN MOTTLED FLINT ENAMEL LION. 1849-1858. Facing right, coleslaw mane, tongue up, marked with 1849 mark A, 9⅜" high, base 11" x 6".

PLATE 376. FLINT ENAMEL LION. 1849-1858. (See also Pl. 377.)

PLATE 377. A DEN OF FLINT ENAMEL LIONS, ALL KNOWN TYPES. 1849-1858. *Top row:* A. Facing right, molded mane, tongue up, with base, marked with 1849 mark A, 8¼" high, base 11" x 6"; B. Facing left, molded mane, tongue down, without base, 7" high. *Center row:* C. Facing right, coleslaw mane, tongue down, without base, 7" high; D. Facing left, coleslaw mane, tongue up, without base, 7" high. *Bottom row:* E. Facing right, coleslaw mane, tongue down, without base, marked with 1849 mark A, 9" high, base 10¾" x 5¾"; F. Facing left, coleslaw mane, tongue up, with base, marked with 1849 mark A, 9" high, base 10¾" x 5¾".

293

PLATE 378. A Dairy of Cows. 1849-1858. A, B, C and D are Rockingham, E, F, G and H are flint enamel. The recumbent cows were made in pairs, facing right and left.

PLATE 379. EXTREMELY RARE FLINT ENAMEL RECUMBENT COW. 1849-1858. Facing right, rare light yellow color, solid coleslaw grass base decorated with applied flowers, no tree stump spill-holder, 5¾″ high, 10″ long.

PLATE 380. FLINT ENAMEL RECUMBENT COW. 1849-1858. Facing right, dark browns and greens, coleslaw tufts of grass, with tree stump spill-holder, 7½″ high, 10″ long.

PLATE 381. FLINT ENAMEL COW CREAMERS. 1849-1858. A. Rare light yellow color, 5⅝" high, 7" long; B. Dark browns and blues, 5¾" high, 7" long. These popular items were made at many potteries. Those made at Bennington can be identified by four features: 1. Open, well-defined eyes, 2. Crescent-shaped nostrils, 3. Ribs can be clearly felt. 4. Folds in neck can be clearly felt. All four points must be present for positive identification.

PLATE 382. TWO EXTREMELY RARE COW CREAMERS. 1850-1858. A. Yellowware, glazed, 5¾" high, 7" long. B. Graniteware, 5½" high, 6⅞" long. No marked cow creamer has been found.

PLATE 383. Two Extremely Rare Cow Creamers. 1850-1858. A. Graniteware, only known example dec- orated with gold, with owner's name on side, 5⅝" high. 1" long; B. Graniteware, 5¾" high, 7" long.

PLATE 384. Only Known Scroddled Ware Cow Creamer. 1853-1858. Shades of brown and cream, small size, 5" high, 6½" long.

PLATE 385. Parian Ornaments with Horses and Cows. 1847-1858. *Top row:* A. Horse, 3¾" high; B. Horse, vase, 5" high. *Bottom row:* C. Recumbent cow, 2⅝" high; D. Cow, 2¾" high.

PLATE 386. Parian Vases and Ornaments with Animals. 1847-1858. *Top row:* A. Deer head, 5¾" high; B. Fox, vase, 5" high. *Bottom row:* C. Recumbent doe, 2⅞" high; D. Sleeping fox, 1⅝" high.

PLATE 387. SMALL PARIAN ORNAMENTS WITH SHEEP. 1847-1858. *Top row:* A. With gold collar, 1⅝″ high; B. Miniature, ¹⁵⁄₁₆″ high, 1⅛″ long; C. 1½″ high. *Bot-tom row:* D. Ram, coleslaw wool, 2¾″ high (See also Pl. 388D.) ; E. Cattail vase, 4¾″ high; F. Ewe, coleslaw wool, 2¾″ high (See also Pl. 388F.)

PLATE 388. PARIAN ORNAMENTS WITH ANIMALS. 1847-1858. *Top row:* A. Recumbent dog and kennel, 3¼″ long; B. Sitting dog, kennel and tree stump, 3½″ high, 3″ diam.; C. Horse on waves with shell on back, 2½″ high, 4⅛″ long. *Bottom row:* D. Recumbent ram, facing right, tree stump, 3¼″ high, 3¼″ long; E. Scratching fox, tree stump, 3¾″ high, 3½″ long; F. Recumbent ewe, facing left, tree stump, 3¼″ high, 3¼″ long. (Compare D and F with Pls. 387D and 387F.)

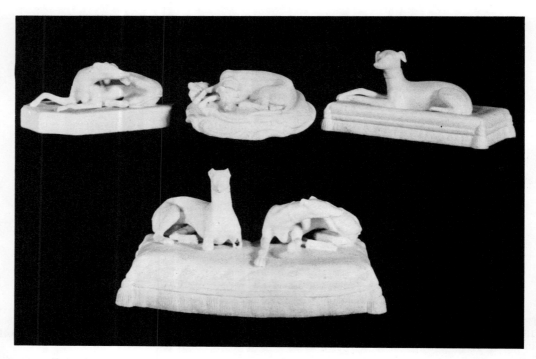

PLATE 389. PARIAN GREYHOUND ORNAMENTS. 1847-1858. *Top row:* A. 2″ high, base 4⅞″ long, 2¾″ wide; B. 1⅝″ high, base 4″ long, 2¾″ wide; C. 2¾″ high, base 5½″ long, 2⅞″ wide. (CAUTION, compare with Pls. 404A, 404B and 404D.) *Bottom row:* D. 4″ high, base 7¼″ long, 4½″ wide. These dogs were also made at many other potteries.

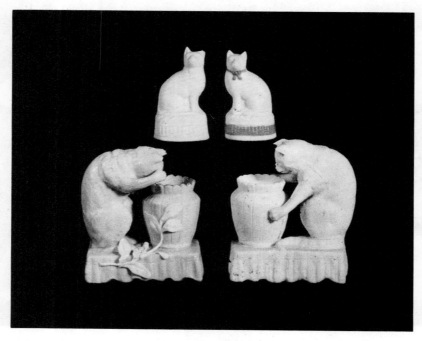

PLATE 390. EXTREMELY RARE PORCELAIN ORNAMENTS WITH CATS. 1850-1858. *Top row:* A. Parian, 3⅛″ high; B. Blue and white porcelain, same design as A, 3″ high. *Bottom row:* C. Extremely rare high-glazed pink porcelain cat, applied Parian flowers on base and urn, 4″ high; D Parian, similar to C, 4¼″ high.

PLATE 391. PARIAN ORNAMENTS AND VASES WITH DOGS. 1847-1858. *Top row:* A. Spaniel, 1⅞″ high; B. Two spaniels, 1½″ high. *Center row:* C. Graniteware spaniel paperweight, same as Pl. 408A; D. Spaniel, tree stump, 2¾″ high; E. Spaniel on cushion, 2¼″ high. *Bottom row:* F. and H. pair. F. Spaniel, facing right, with sheaf of wheat vase, 2″ high, oval base, 4″ long, 2½″ wide; G. Two spaniels, glazed polka dots, 5½″ high; H. Spaniel, facing left, 4″ high.

PLATE 393. PARIAN VASES WITH BIRDS. 1847-1858. *Top row:* A. and C. Pair. A. Rooster, 5″ high; B. Parrot, 9¼″ high; C. Hen, 4¾″ high. *Bottom row:* D. and E. Pair, peacock, 9¼″ high.

PLATE 392. HANGING PARIAN BIRD ORNAMENT. 1847-1858. Extremely rare specimen, made to be suspended from above, 7½″ long from beak to tail.

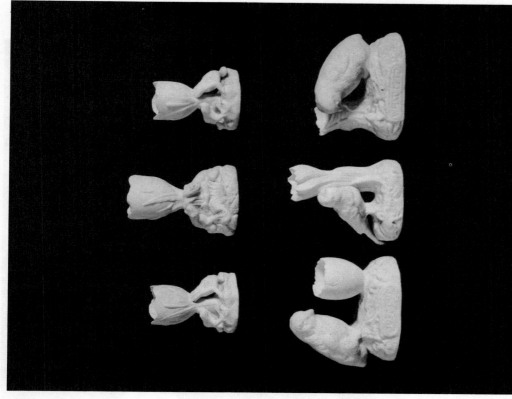

PLATE 395. SMALL PARIAN VASES WITH FROGS, CHICKS. 1847-1858. *Top row:* A. and C. Pair, two frogs at base of crocus, 3¼" high; B. Frogs and crocus, 4" high. *Bottom row:* D. Chick and shell, incised at base "JUST OUT," 4" high; E. Sparrow and crocus, 4" high; F. Chick and frog, incised at base, "WHAT IS IT," 3¼" high.

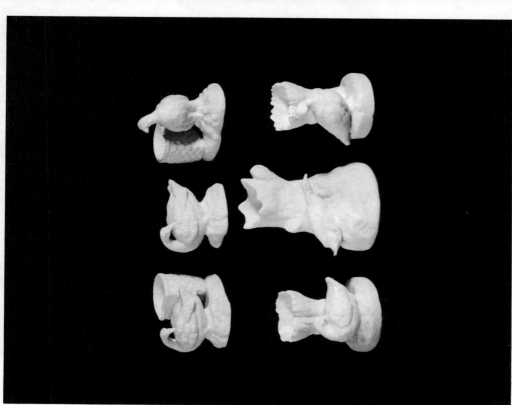

PLATE 394. SMALL PARIAN ORNAMENTS WITH GEESE, PARTRIDGE. 1847-1858. *Top row:* A. Goose, 2⅛" high; B. Goose, 2⅛" high; C. Partridge, 2⅞" high. *Bottom row:* D. Goose, sheaf of wheat, 2⅝" high; E. Goose, tree stump, 4" high; F. Goose, sheaf of wheat, 2⅝" high.

303

PLATE 396. PARIAN ORNAMENTS AND VASES WITH SWANS. 1847-1858. *Top row:* A. 4½″ high; B. 4″ high. *Bottom row:* C. Rare vase, 9″ high; D. 7″ high.

PLATE 397. EXTREMELY RARE GRANITEWARE SWAN. 1850-1858. Decorated with cobalt blue on base and in eye, wings applied to body, body to base, 5¼" high, 5¼" long.

PLATE 398. EXTREMELY RARE SMEAR-GLAZED SWAN. 1850-1858. 5¼" long.

PLATE 399. EAGLE FORMS, VARIOUS ITEMS. 1850-1858.
Top row: A. Graniteware paperweight, 2¾" high, base 4" long 2½" wide (See also Pl. 408B.); B. Parian ornament, eagle and child, 4½" high. (See also Pl. 354B.)

Bottom row: C. Eagle vase, Parian body with applied color glazes, blue-green stripe on base, pink and gold on vase, 7⅜" high (See also Pl. 401.); D. Parian vase, 7½" high. (See also Pl. 401.)

PLATE 400. Rare Parian Eagle Vases. 1847-1858. A. Top of urn has obviously been ground off, 8½″ high as is; B. Same design, rare small size, 7½″ high.

PLATE 401. Eagle Vases. 1847-1858. A. Extremely rare Belleek vase, 6½″ high; B. Same as 399C, 7⅜″ high.

CHAPTER SEVEN: NOVELTY ITEMS

From the collector's point of view, the various toby forms produced at Bennington almost rival the well-known animal figures in poularity. From the variety of such items it can be seen that they were popular production items.

Toby snuff jars and toby bottles were made in several different sizes, and toby pitchers were made in five different patterns. The popular book flasks, which were made in three sizes, are likely to be confused at first glance with those produced elsewhere. An aid to identification, although it is not always present, is a small rim of beaded dots around the opening at the top. If the flask bears a title with the word "Bennington" in it, such as *Bennington Battle, Bennington Ladies* or *Bennington Companion,* it is obviously a Bennington-made article.

Many of the novelty items must be studied closely for details, as similar items are known to have been produced elsewhere. The coin banks, especially the English cottage one, were not made in quantity at Bennington but were a popular production item in English potteries.

Special note should be taken of the items which have a majolica-like glaze. This glaze is usually associated only with the hanging flower pots made by the Norton Pottery. These majolica examples are the only patterns known to have been made in this finish at the Fenton Pottery. They never passed the experimental stage and are unusual specimens.

Included in this section also are miniature items, toys and accessories, including tiny pitchers, vases and jugs and the exceptionally lovely Parian flower pieces. These dainty baskets are extremely rare, since they were made only on special order. They were among the first pieces of Parian porcelain produced in America. John Harrison, a modeler from the Copeland Works in England, is known to have made a few of these at the Fenton Pottery. Harrison-made items, which are considered to be among the most desirable Parian pieces, are limited in number and difficult to document.

PLATE 402. ONLY KNOWN EXAMPLE YELLOWWARE
TOBY SNUFF JAR. 1849-1858. Marked with 1849 mark
A, 5¼" high. (See also Pl. 417.)

PLATE 403. EXTREMELY RARE STONEWARE INKSTAND. 1841. Mentioned in an advertisement by Julius Norton dated February 27, 1841. Decorated with cobalt blue, 3½" high, base 7" long, 4¼" wide. (CAUTION, compare with Pl. 404.)

PLATE 404. COMPARISON PIECES, NOTE CAREFULLY. *Top row:* A and B. Pair of redware greyhounds, lead-glazed, known to have been made in West Sterling, Mass., 2½" high, base 6" long, 3" wide. *Bottom row:* C. Stoneware inkwell, made by Julius Norton, 1841, 3½" high, base 7" long, 4¼" wide. (See also Pl. 403.) Compare with D, made by and marked, Walley, Smith and Skinner, England. Red clay covered with black slip in imitation of basalt, identical in design to C, slightly larger in size, 4" high, base 7¾" long, 4¾" wide.

PLATE 405. RARE GRANITEWARE INKWELL, PHRENO-
LOGICAL HEAD. 1850-1859. A. Side view, skull marked
with black, base with gold, 5½″ high; B. Front view,
base marked with cobalt blue, 5½″ high.

PLATE 406. ROCKINGHAM AND FLINT ENAMEL INK-WELLS. 1853-1858. *Top row:* A. Day and Night pattern, Rockingham, coleslaw decoration applied on top, extremely rare, 4½" high (See also Pls. 93A, 93B and 93C); B. Early Rockingham lion inkwell, 2½" high, 4¾" long; C. Rockingham dome inkwell, 3¾" high. *Bottom row:* D. Flint enamel, top removable, 3" high; E. Early Rockingham lion head, also made in gold decorated graniteware, 3½" high; F. Flint enamel, inserts removable, 2½" high, 4" long, 3½" wide.

PLATE 407. FLINT ENAMEL PAPERWEIGHTS. 1849-1858. Marked with 1849 mark A. *Top row:* A. Rectangular, 2⅜" high, base 5⅛" long, 3¼" wide. *Bottom row:* B. Reverse of spaniel-topped paperweight, 3" high, base 4½" long, 2¾" wide; C. Obverse of B, same dimensions.

PLATE 408. GRANITEWARE PAPERWEIGHTS. 1850-1858.
A. Spaniel-topped, this weight is sometimes decorated
in black. 1⅞″ high, base 4″ long, 2½″ wide; B. Eagle-
topped, extremely rare with gold decoration, 2¾″ high,
base 4″ long, 2½″ wide.

PLATES 409 and 409A. EXTREMELY RARE ROCKING-HAM DESK SET. 1854. Bottom is an inkwell with re-movable corner decorations, next section was probably used for sealing wax, shaker held blotting sand, top was a steeple-shaped finial or cap. 12½" assembled height.

PLATE 410. MARKED SCRODDLED WARE BOOK FLASK. 1847-1849. Only known example with applied star on spine. (For similar stars on globe see also Pl. 15.)

Note unique use of Fenton's Works mark E. Rare gray and pink, 10½″ high, 8″ wide, 3″ thick.

315

PLATE 411. BOOK FLASKS. 1849-1858. Made in three sizes, 4-qt., 2-qt., 1-pt., these flasks were popular novelty items made in both Rockingham and flint enamel in all sizes. They frequently have titles impressed on the spine such as: *Battle of Bennington, Bennington Ladies, Hermit's Delight, Suffering and Death, Life of Kossuth* and many others. When they are marked, it is usually with 1849 mark A or small 1849 mark C, and extremely rarely Fenton's Works mark E. A. 11" high; B. 8" high; C. Extremely rare example in brown slip-covered stoneware, marked "NORTON, 1873," 8" high; D. 5½" high.

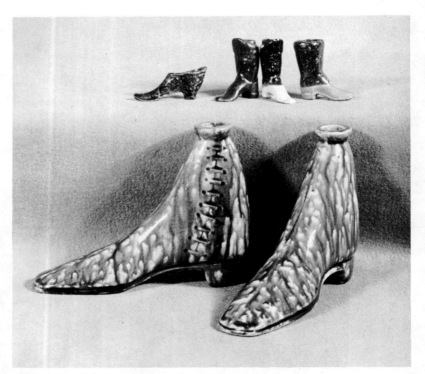

PLATE 412. ROCKINGHAM BOOTS AND SHOES. 1849-1858. *Top row:* A. Shoe, ⅞" high, 2¼" long; B. Boot, solid Rockingham, 2" high; C. Boot, white foot, 2" high; D. Boot, yellow foot, 2" high. A, B, C and D were all made by the Bennington potter William Leake. *Bottom row:* E and F. Rockingham, pair, laces on opposite sides, 5" high, 6" long.

316

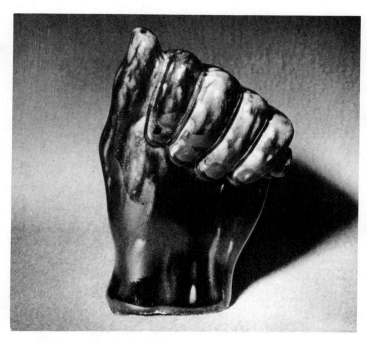

PLATE 413. Novelty Flint Enamel Clenched Fist. 1849-1858. Only known example, use unknown, lovely blue and brown coloring, hollow, lightweight, 4″ high.

PLATE 414. Extremely Rare Graniteware Hand Dish. 1850-1858. A pattern familiar in opaque glass, this dish is made of thin graniteware, one leaf broken, 7″ long, 5″ wide.

PLATE 415. EXTREMELY RARE SCRODDLED WARE TOBY PITCHER. 1853-1858. Marked with U.S.P. "oval" mark H, 6¼″ high. All scroddled ware is rare, but especially so in toby pitchers.

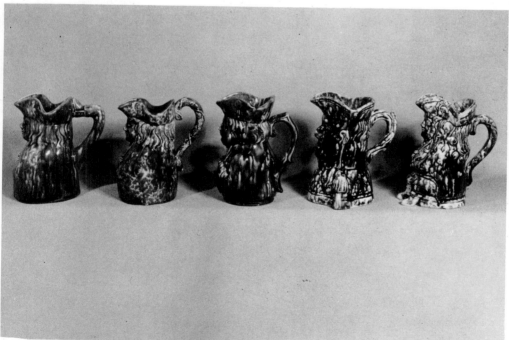

PLATES 416 and 416A. TOBY PITCHERS. 1849-1858. Front and side views of the five Bennington-made designs. All have a flat bottom, rather than a highly concave one, which is characteristic of most examples of toby pitchers from other potteries. A. Ben Franklin pattern, boot handle, 5¾″ high; B. Ben Franklin, grape-vine handle, 5¾″ high; C. Standard toby, 5⅞″ high; D. General Stark, 6″ high, rare; E. Sitting toby, grape-vine handle, 6⅛″ high. A, B and E were made both in Rockingham and flint enamel, and marked with 1849 mark A; C and D are only known to have been made in Rockingham; E. Also made in scroddled ware.

PLATE 417. Rare Toby Snuff Jars. 1849-1858. *Top row:* A. Flint enamel, marked with 1849 mark A, 4¼" high; B. Brown slip-covered, marked with U.S.P. "ribbon" mark F, 3⅞" high; C. Flint enamel, light green, marked with 1849 mark A, 4¼" high. *Bottom row:* D. Same as Pl. 402; E. Extremely rare change cover, no bottom, 4¼" high; F. Extremely rare type on base, marked with 1849 mark A, 5¼" high.

PLATE 418. TOBY SNUFF JARS. 1849-1858. Marked with 1849 mark A. Usually the hats come off and serve as covers. A. Hat made on body, slot in back, 4¼″ high; B. Rare olive-green flint enamel, 4¼″ high.

PLATE 419. RARE TOBY BOTTLES, THREE SIZES. 1847-1858. A. 10½″ high; B. 9¾″ high; C. Extremely rare size, 8½″ high. (Compare with Pls. 420, 421 and 423.)

PLATE 421. RARE TOBY BOTTLES. 1847-1858. A. Flint enamel, holding mug, no tassels, marked with 1849 mark A, 10½″ high; B. Brown slip-covered, holding mug, no tassels, 9½″ high; C. Flint enamel, holding bottle, tassels, mustache, marked with 1849 mark A, 10¾″ high.

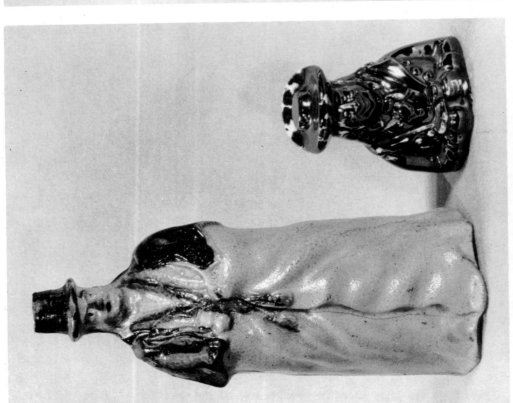

PLATE 420. ONLY KNOWN EXAMPLES TOBY ITEMS. 1849-1858. A. Stoneware with cobalt decoration, peculiarly marked with 1849 mark A, small size, 9¼″ high; B. Change cover, no bottom, flint enamel, 3¾″ high. (Compare hat with Pl. 417E.)

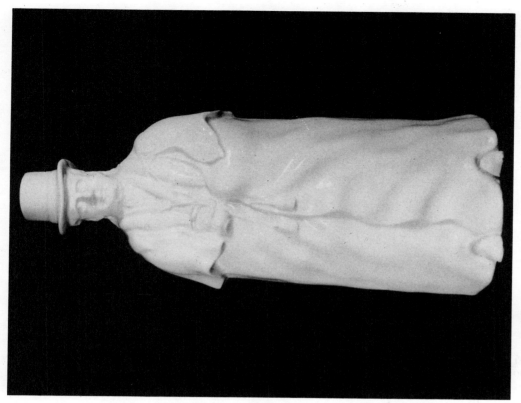

PLATE 423. ONLY KNOWN EXAMPLE GRANITEWARE TOBY BOTTLE. 1850-1858. With tassels, feet showing, 11½" high.

PLATE 422. EXTREMELY RARE TOBY BARREL BOTTLES. 1849-1858. Impressed with 1849 mark A. A. Flint enamel, barrel incised with script initials "G.G.," 11" high; B. Rockingham, barrel impressed "Old Tom," small size, 8" high; C. Flint enamel, barrel has applied letters "BILL," 11" high.

323

PLATE 424. FLINT ENAMEL COVERED TOBY HEAD. 1849-1858. Only known example, tri-cornered hat a separate cover, cream-colored inside, marked with 1849 mark A, 6½″ over-all, 5″ without hat.

PLATE 425. FLINT ENAMEL ZACHARY TAYLOR PITCHERS. 1849-1858. Rare, "Rough" on one side, "Ready" on reverse, in ribbon scroll on hat, 13¼″ high.

PLATE 426. EXTREMELY RARE FLINT ENAMEL SWISS LADY. 1849-1858. Light green with cream-colored face and yellow hair, no bottom, hoop skirt used as a cover over coins on a bar counter, 7″ high.

PLATE 427. ONLY KNOWN EXAMPLE FLINT ENAMEL SWISS LADY BANK. 1849-1858. No hat, slot in skirt, bottom marked with 1849 mark A, 6½″ high.

PLATE 428. BANKS. 1847-1855. *Top row:* A. Rockingham chest of drawers, 3″ high; B. Flint enamel Uncle Sam head, 4½″ high; C. Rockingham cottage, 6½″ high.

PLATE 429. BANKS. 1847-1877. *Top row:* A. Brown slip-covered stoneware, owner's name, "EDDIE NORTON," impressed on rim, 6¾″ high. *Bottom row:* B. Flint enamel, 4¾″ high; C. Early Rockingham, 5½″ high.

PLATE 430. BLUE AND WHITE PORCELAIN FRAGMENTS OF A HEAD. 1850-1858. Only known example, 2¾″ high. Intended to be used on handle of a cane, these fragments were dug up at site of Fenton's pottery.

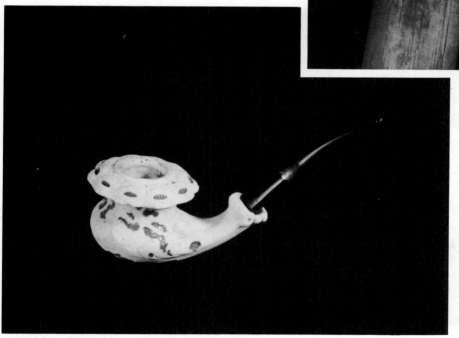

PLATE 431. ONLY KNOWN EXAMPLE BLUE AND WHITE PORCELAIN PIPE. 1850-1858. Silver ferrule, amber stem, obviously made and used by one of the potters, not a production item. Over-all length 6″; porcelain section, 3½″ long; outside bowl, 2″ diam.

PLATE 432. EXTREMELY RARE PARIAN BASKET OF FLOWERS. 1853-1858. Extremely fine specimen, incorporating most of known flower forms used at Bennington, 3¼" high.

PLATE 433. JOHN HARRISON'S BASKETS WITH APPLIED FLOWERS. 1843-1845. The only two positively identified Parian pieces known to have been made by John Harrison. There are about three other known baskets which probably were made by him. A. Parian, same design as B, except fruit and flowers replace baby. Presented to a Bennington lady in December, 1843, by John Harrison. B. Presented by John Harrison to Julius Norton's wife, Eliza, on the occasion of the birth of the Nortons' first child, December, 1843. Traditional deep blue-gray associated only with Harrison, unglazed porcelain. Both, 1⅛" high, 3½" long, 2¼" wide.

PLATE 434. EXTREMELY RARE PARIAN MINIATURE BASKETS OF APPLIED FLOWERS. These were not production items, but were made for special orders. *Top row:* A and B. Without handles. *Bottom row:* C and D. With handles; E. With handle, scattered "Harrison Blue" flowers. B and E could probably be attributed to John Harrison. Largest size, 2″ high, 2″ long; smallest size, 1″ high, 1″ long.

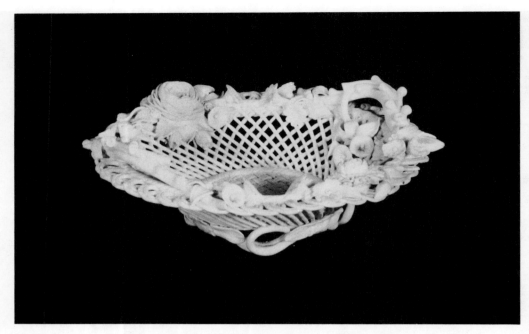

PLATE 435. Rare Parian Basket with Applied Flowers. 1847-1858. Perfect example, same as 436B, 2″ high, 7½″ diam.

PLATE 436. Rare Parian Baskets with Applied Decoration. 1847-1858. *Top row:* A. Solid basket-shaped, grapes on sides and handle, 6½″ high, 5½″ diam. *Bottom row:* B. Extremely fine latticework basket with ap-plied flowers, part of rim broken, 2″ high, 7½″ diam.; C. Extremely rare diamond-shaped latticework basket with applied flowers, part of rim broken, 2″ high, 8″ long.

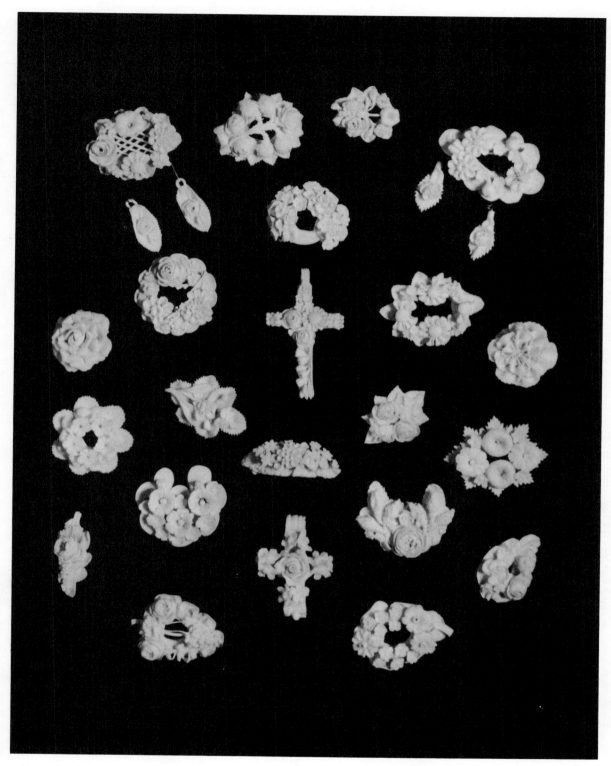

PLATE 437. RARE PARIAN JEWELRY WITH APPLIED FLOWERS. 1847-1858. Similar jewelry items were made in various English potteries. These pieces, which incorporate characteristic Bennington flowers, include brooches, crosses, pendants, earrings, stickpins and bracelet pieces for ribbon ties.

PLATE 438. Rare Parian Sewing Accessories. 1847-1859. *Top row:* A. Needle and thread case, 2¼″ high, 2¾″ diam.; B. Pincushion, 1″ high, 2″ diam.; C. Pin-holder, 2¾″ high, 2″ diam. *Bottom row:* D. Pincushion, 1⅝″ high, 3″ diam.; E. Pincushion, 2⅜″ high, 4¼″ diam.; F. Pincushion, 1½″ high, 3″ diam.

PLATE 439. PARIAN NOVELTY ITEMS. 1847-1858. *Top row:* A. Darning egg, Negro boy breaking through shell, 2½″ long. Plain nest eggs used in the chicken nest were also made. B. Candle snuffer, squirrel finial, also made in blue and white porcelain, 3¾″ high; C. Bird in coleslaw nest, 1⅝″ high. *Bottom row:* D. Hand, 3¾″ high; E. Hand, 5⅛″ high; F. Boots, 3¼″ high.

PLATE 440. EXTREMELY RARE MAJOLICA-TYPE AND PARIAN ITEMS. 1847-1858. These were purely experimental and made only in limited quantities. *Top row:* A, B and C, pineapple-shaped pitchers. A. Highly-glazed porcelain, 3¾″ high; B. Majolica-type, 3¾″ high; C. Parian, 3¾″ high. *Bottom row:* D, E and F, Molded Grapevine pattern, scalloped top. D. Majolica-type, light, 4″ high; E. Parian, 4″ high; F. Majolica-type, dark, 4″ high.

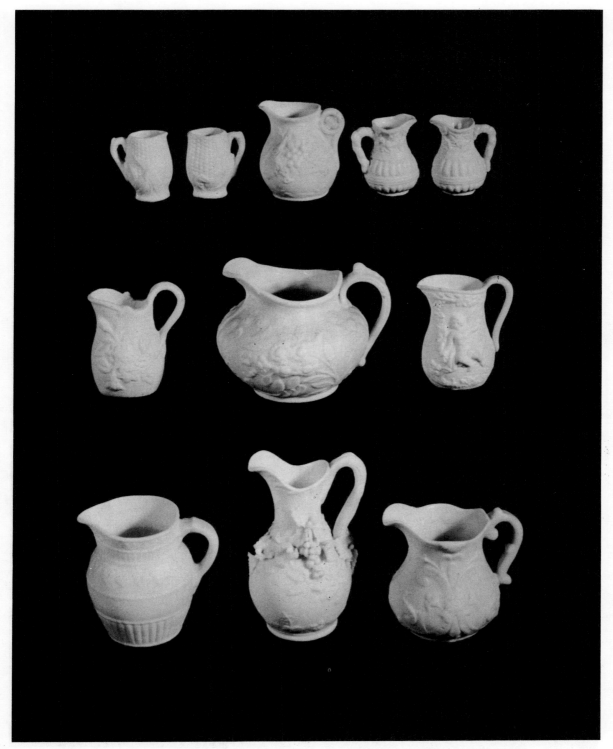

PLATE 441. MINIATURE PARIAN PORCELAIN PITCHERS. 1847-1858. *Top row:* A. and B. 1⅝″ high; C. 2¼″ high; D. and E. 1⅞″ high. (See also Pl. 103B.) *Center row:* F. 2½″ high; G. 3″ high; H. 2½″ high. *Bottom row:* I. 2¾″ high; J. Applied grape decoration, 4″ high; K. 3″ high.

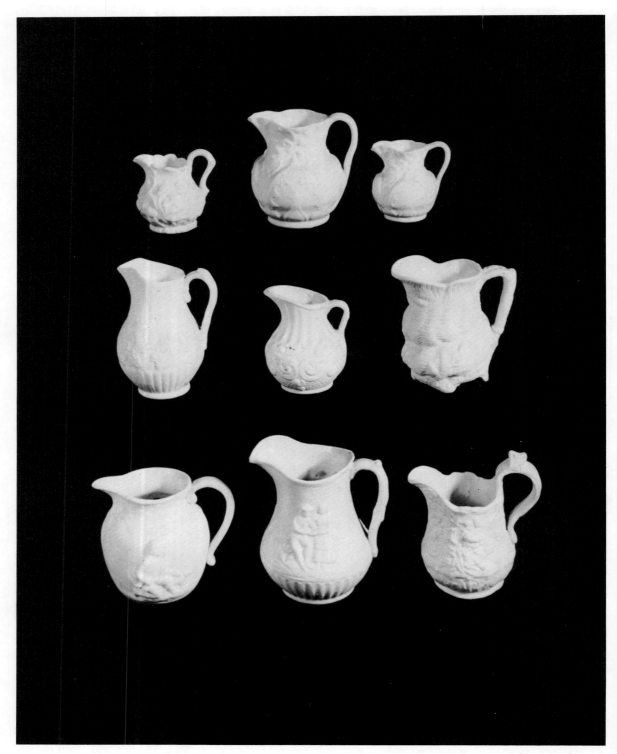

PLATE 442. MINIATURE PARIAN PORCELAIN PITCHERS. 1847-1858. Top row: A. 2¼″ high; B. 3⅛″ high; C. 2⅛″ high. *Center row:* D. 3⅞″ high; E. 2⅞″ high; F. Shell pattern, 3½″ high. *Bottom row:* G. 3¾″ high; H. 4¼″ high; I. 4″ high.

336

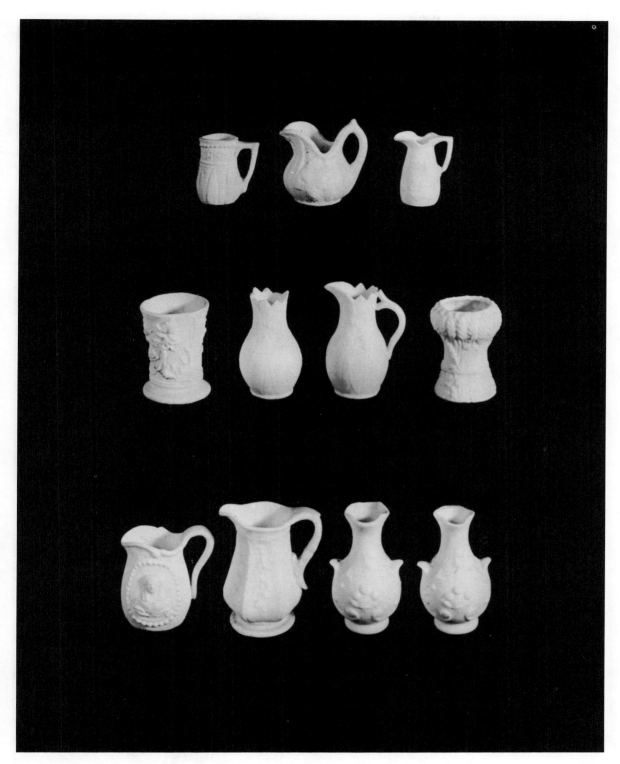

PLATE 443. MINIATURE PARIAN VASES AND PITCHERS. 1847-1858. *Top row:* A. 1⅝" high; B. 2" high; C. 1¾" high. *Center row:* D. 2¼" high; E. Same as F without handle, 2½" high; F. same as E with handle, 2⅝" high; G. 2¼" high; (See also Pl. 249F.) *Bottom row:* H. 2¼" high; I. 3" high (See also Pl. 105E.); J. and K. Pair, 2⅞" high.

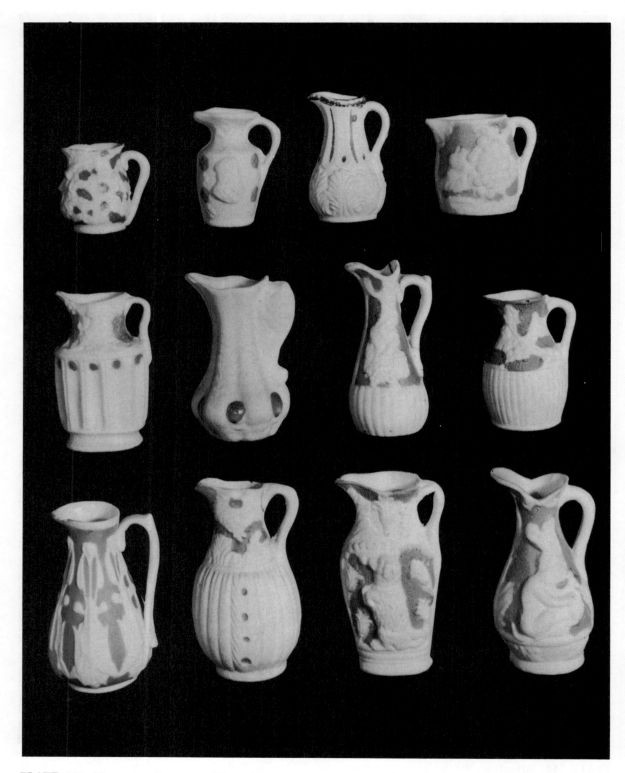

PLATE 444. MINIATURE BLUE AND WHITE PORCELAIN PITCHERS. 1850-1858. *Top row:* A. 1¾″ high; B. 2″ high; C. 2⅛″ high; D. 1⅞″ high. *Center row:* E. 2¾″ high; F. 3⅛″ high; G. 3¼″ high; H. 2⅜″ high. *Bottom row:* I. 3¼″ high; J. 3¾″ high; K. 3¾″ high; L. 3¾″ high.

338

PLATE 445. Miniature Blue and White Porcelain Vases. 1850-1858. *Top row:* A. 2¼″ high; B. 2¼″ high; C. 2⅜″ high. *Center row:* D. 3″ high; E. 4″ high; F. 2½″ high. *Bottom row:* G. 4″ high; H. 3¾″ high; I. 4″ high.

PLATE 446. Rare Parian Toy Tea Set. 1847-1858.
Cups, 1⅛″ high, 1½″ diam.; Saucer, 2½″ diam.; Sugar
bowl, 2″ high; Teapot, 2″ high.

PLATE 447. Rare Common White Pottery Toy Tea
Set. Only known example, this set was made for a
little Bennington girl. A. Pitcher, 3½″ high; B. Teapot,
5¾″ high; C. Sugar bowl, 4¾″ high.

PLATE 448. ONLY KNOWN EXAMPLE BROWN SLIP-COVERED TOY DISHES. Made by John Harrison for the daughter of his landlady. A Sugar bowl, 1⅞″ high; B. Cup, 1⅛″ high, Saucer, 3¼″ diam.; C. Pitcher, 2″ high.

PLATE 449. MINIATURE STONEWARE CROCKS, COBALT-DECORATED. A. 3″ high; B. 1850-1859, marked "J. & E. Norton," 3½″ high; C. 3¼″ high.

PLATE 450. MINIATURE ROCKINGHAM AND FLINT ENAMEL ITEMS. *Top row:* A. Rockingham cuspidor, 1½″ high; B. 12 tiny jugs, ½″ to 1⅞″ high; C. Brown slip-covered cup and saucer; cup, 1¼″ high, 2″ diam., saucer, 3½″ diam. (See also Pl. 448.) *Bottom row:* D. Flint enamel goblet, 2½″ high; E. Rockingham footed bowl, 2¼″ high; F. Rockingham pitcher, 3⅛″ high, bowl, 1⅝″ high; G. Rockingham jardiniere, 2¼″ high.

342

LIST OF ILLUSTRATIONS

Color Plates   PAGE

A. Variety of Bennington Ware   188A
B. Flint Enamel Washbowl and Pitcher   188B
C. Lamps with Flint Enamel Bases   188C
D. Ewers, Vase, Pitchers and Trinket Box   188D
E. Blue and White Porcelain Ewer   188E
F. Cobalt-Decorated Stoneware Inkwell   188F
G. Toby or Coachman Bottles   188F

Halftone Plates   PAGE

1. Omindia Gerry Jug   3
2. Early Norton Pottery Pieces
3. Early Redware Jug   4-5
4. Brown Slip-Covered Stoneware Jar
5. Norton Stoneware Jug and Crocks
6. Norton Stoneware Jugs and Pitcher
7. Extremely Rare Stoneware Covered and Footed Bowl   6-7
8. Extremely Rare Stoneware Jug with Applied Eagle
9. Norton Stoneware Crocks
10. Elaborate Stoneware Water Cooler
11. Elaborate Cobalt-Decorated Stoneware Jug
12. Presentation Stoneware Jug, Cobalt Decoration   8
13. Presentation Stoneware Jug, Cobalt Decoration
14. Presentation Stoneware Jug, Cobalt Decoration
15. Parian Statue and Statuettes   16
16. Famous Monument Exhibited in New York
17. Famous Flint Enamel Standing Stag   17
18. Flint Enamel Apostle Pattern Water Cooler
19. Parian Clock Case   18
20. Extremely Rare Parian Flower Centerpiece
21. Wild Rose Pattern Pitcher   23
22. Early Rockingham (or Dark-Luster) Pitchers   24-25
23. Early Rockingham Pitchers
24. Flint Enamel Pitchers   26-27
25. Rockingham and Flint Enamel Pitchers
26. Flint Enamel and Rockingham Pitchers
27. Rockingham and Flint Enamel Pitchers
28. Barrel-Shaped Pitchers   28-29
29. Flint Enamel and Rockingham Pitchers
30. Diamond Pattern Flint Enamel Pitchers
31. Diamond Pattern Rockingham Pitcher
32. Hound-Handled Pitcher   30-31
33. Hound-Handled Pitchers
34. Hound-Handled Pitchers   32-33
35. Comparison Pieces: Hound-Handled Pitchers
36. Comparison Pieces: Hound-Handled Pitchers
37. Comparison Pieces: Hound-Handled Pitchers
38. Scroddled Ware Pitchers   34-35
39. Diamond Pattern Scroddled Ware Pitchers
40. Graniteware Banded Pitcher
41. Graniteware Pitcher
42. "Sweetheart" or "Presentation" Pitcher   36-37
43. "Sweetheart" or "Presentation" Pitcher
44 and 44A. "Sweetheart" or "Presentation" Pitchers

   PAGE

45. "Sweetheart" or "Presentation" Pitcher   38-39
46. "Sweetheart" or "Presentation" Pitcher and Matching Cup
47. "Sweetheart" or "Presentation" Pitchers
48. "Sweetheart" or "Presentation" Pitchers
49. Comparison Pieces: Presentation Pitchers
50. Cascade Pattern Pitcher   40-41
51. Cascade Pattern Pitchers
52. Charter Oak Pattern Pitcher
53. Charter Oak Pattern Pitchers
54. Cherub and Grapes Pattern Pitchers   42-43
55. Corn Husk Pattern Pitchers
56. Cupid and Psyche Pattern Pitcher   44-45
57. Cupid and Psyche Pattern Pitchers
58. Daffodil Pattern Parian Pitchers   46-47
59. Geometric Arabesque Pattern Pitchers
60. The Good Samaritan Pattern Pitcher
61. Comparison Pieces: The Good Samaritan Pattern
62. Ivy Vine Pattern Pitcher   48-49
63. Ivy Vine Pattern Pitcher
64. Lily Pad Pattern Pitchers
65. Love and War Pattern Parian Pitcher   50-51
66. Comparison Pieces: Love and War Pattern
67. Parian Porcelain Pitcher
68. Paneled Grapevine Pitchers
69. Paneled Grapevine Pitchers   52-53
70. Two Rare-Patterned Pitchers
71. Paneled Vine and Flower Pattern Pitchers
72. Paul and Virginia Pattern Pitcher   54-55
73. Paul and Virginia Pattern Pitcher
74. Comparison Pieces: Paul and Virginia Pattern   56-57
75. Comparison Pieces: Paul and Virginia Pattern
76. Paul and Virginia Pattern Pitchers   58-59
77. Two Gray-Green Porcelain Pitchers
78. Pond Lily Pattern Pitcher   60-61
79. Comparison Piece: Pond Lily Pattern
80. Pond Lily Pattern Pitchers   62-63
81. Pond Lily Pattern Pitchers
82. Pond Lily Pattern Pitcher   64-65
83. Pond Lily and Acanthus Leaf Pattern Pitcher
84. Snowdrop Pattern Parian Pitchers   66-67
85. Comparison Pieces: Snowdrop Pattern
86. Tulip and Sunflower Pattern Pitcher   68-69
87. Tulip and Sunflower Pattern Pitcher
88. Tulip and Sunflower Pattern Pitchers   70-71
89. Tulip and Sunflower Pattern Pitchers
90. Tulip and Sunflower Pattern and Wild Rose Pattern Pitchers   72-73
91. Comparison Pieces: Tulip and Sunflower Pattern
92. Wild Rose Pattern Pitchers
93. Blue and White Porcelain Pitchers   74-75
94. Blue and White Porcelain Pitchers
95. Blue and White Porcelain Pitchers
96. Blue and White Porcelain Pitchers
97. Palm Tree Pattern Syrup Pitchers   76-77
98. Palm Tree Pattern Pitcher
99. Bird and Nest Pattern Syrup Pitchers
100. Palm Tree Pattern Syrup Pitchers
101. Graniteware Syrup Pitchers
102. Parian Porcelain Pitchers   78-79
103. Parian Porcelain Pitchers
104. Parian and White Porcelain Pitchers

   PAGE

105. Parian and White Porcelain Pitchers
106. Parian Porcelain Pitchers   80-81
107. Parian Porcelain Pitchers
108. Parian and White Porcelain Pitchers
109. Rare Flint Enamel Covered Coffee Urn   83
110. Cupid and Psyche Pattern Sugar Bowls and Teapots   84-85
111. Extremely Rare Parian Tea Set
112. Parian Morning Glory Pattern Sugar Bowl and Creamer   86-87
113. Parian Paneled Vine and Flower Pattern Sugar Bowl and Creamer
114. Assorted Parian Table Pieces
115. Rare Parian Pond Lily Pattern Cups and Saucers   88-89
116. Assorted Parian Table Pieces
117. Assorted Parian Pond Lily Pattern Table Pieces
118. Assorted Parian Table Pieces
119. Graniteware Fruit Baskets   90-91
120. Part of a White Porcelain Tea Service
121. Part of a White Porcelain Tea Service
122. Part of a White Porcelain Tea Service
123. Rare Rockingham Covered Bowl   92-93
124. Extremely Rare Rockingham Covered Dish
125. Extremely Rare Flint Enamel Table Articles
126. Flint Enamel Sugar Bowls
127. Covered Tobacco Jars   94-95
128. Covered Rockingham Tobacco Jar
129. Alternate Rib Pattern Tobacco Jars
130. Covered Tobacco Jars
131. Rockingham Beakers and Goblets   96-97
132. Rockingham Footed Goblets
133. Rockingham Beakers and Mugs
134. Rockingham Handled Mugs
135. Rare Complete Flint Enamel Tea and Coffee Service   98-99
136. Two Flint Enamel Coffeepots
137. Flint Enamel Teapots
138. Rockingham and Flint Enamel Teapots
139. Extremely Rare Rockingham Teapot   100-101
140. Alternate Rib Pattern Flint Enamel Teapot
141. Common Brown Slip-Ware Shaving Mug   103
142. Rockingham Pipkins, with Covers   104-105
143. Rockingham, Yellowware and Flint Enamel Pipkins
144. Flint Enamel and Rockingham Bowls and Molds
145. Rockingham Cake Molds
146. Flint Enamel and Rockingham Pie Plates and Baking Dishes   106-107
147. Comparison Pieces: Rockingham Oval Bakers
148. Rockingham Kitchen Accessories
149. Rockingham Mixing Bowls
150. Common Yellowware Bowls   108-109
151. Mortar and Pestles in Mortar or Wedgwood Ware
152. Norton Stoneware Churns   110-111
153. Norton Stoneware Items, No Decoration
154. Brown Slip-Covered Stoneware Pitchers
155. Brown Slip-Covered Stoneware Items
156. Brown Slip-Covered Stoneware Items

Halftone Plates *(continued)*

	PAGE
157. Flint Enamel Washbasin	112-113
158. Rare Rockingham Washboard	
159. Rockingham Croup Kettles or Inhalators	
160. Flint Enamel Water Cooler	114-115
161. Rockingham Water Coolers	
162. Graniteware Shaving Mugs	
163. Rockingham and Graniteware Soap Dishes	116-117
164. Rockingham and Flint Enamel Soap Dishes and Toilet Boxes	
165. Flint Enamel Soap Dishes and Toilet Boxes	
166. Flint Enamel Diamond Pattern Washbowl and Pitcher	118-119
167. Flint Enamel Scalloped Rib Pattern Washbowl and Pitcher	
168. Flint Enamel Scroll Edge Washbowl and Pitcher	
169. Flint Enamel Alternate Rib Pattern Washbowl and Pitcher	
170. Extremely Rare Scroddled Ware Washbowl and Pitcher	120-121
171. Graniteware Gold-Decorated Washbowl and Pitcher	
172. Graniteware Gold- and Blue-Decorated Washbowl and Pitcher	122-123
173. Graniteware Gold- and Blue-Decorated Toilet Set	
174. Graniteware Decorated Chamber Pots	
175. Flint Enamel Chamber Pot and Bedpans	
176. Graniteware Gold- and Blue-Decorated Slop Jar	124-125
177. Extremely Rare Scroddled Ware Diamond Pattern Slop Jar	
178. Rare Flint Enamel Scalloped Rib Pattern Slop Jars	
179. Rare Rockingham Slop Jar and Bowl	
180. Scalloped Rib Pattern Foot Baths	126-127
181. Graniteware Decorated Foot Baths	
182. Extremely Rare Graniteware Foot Warmer	
183. Rockingham and Flint Enamel Foot Warmers	
184. Flint Enamel and Rockingham Cuspidors	128-129
185. Rockingham and Flint Enamel Cuspidors	
186. Extremely Rare Scroddled Ware Cuspidors	
187. Comparison Pieces: Cuspidors	
188. Rockingham and Flint Enamel Jardinieres	130-131
189. Rockingham Jardinieres	
190. Rockingham Jardinieres	
191. Brown Slip-Covered Flower Pots	
192. Rare Biscuit-Fired Scroll Support	132-133
193. Extremely Rare Flint Enamel Scroll Supports	
194. Rare Flint Enamel Tiles and Ceiling Decoration	
195. Rare Flint Enamel Dish Candleholders	134-135
196. Rockingham and Flint Enamel Candlesticks	
197. Rockingham and Flint Enamel Candlesticks	
198. Rockingham and Flint Enamel Candlesticks	
199. Door Knobs and Drawer Pulls	136-137
200. Rare Flint Enamel and Rockingham Curtain Tie-Backs	
201. Extremely Rare Parian Curtain Tie-Backs	
202. Graniteware Accessories	
203. Rockingham and Flint Enamel Name Plates	138-139
204. Flint Enamel Picture Frames	
205. Extremely Rare Parian Keyhole Cover	

	PAGE
206. Parian Name Plates and Alphabet Letters	
207. Extremely Rare Flint Enamel Lamp Base	140-141
208. Rare Flint Enamel Lamp Base	
209. Extremely Rare Parian Cologne Bottle	143
210. Two Crude Vases or Spill-Holders	144-145
211. Graniteware Banded Vases	
212. Rare Rockingham and Flint Enamel Vases	
213. Flint Enamel Tulip Vases	146-147
214. Extremely Rare Tulip Vases	
215. Scroddled Ware Cottage-Type Vase	
216. Extremely Rare Cottage-Type Vases	148-149
217. Extremely Rare Cottage-Type Vases	
218. Extremely Rare Cottage-Type Vases	
219. Blue and White Porcelain Vases, Victoria and Albert Pattern	150-151
220. Parian Porcelain Vases, Victoria and Albert Pattern	
221. Parian Porcelain Vases, Portrait Medallion	
222. Blue and White Porcelain Vases, Portrait Medallion	
223. Extremely Rare Pair of Pink and White Porcelain Vases	152-153
224. Extremely Rare Pair of Green and White Porcelain Vases	
225. Extremely Rare Belleek-Type Porcelain Vases	
226. Parian Body Vase with Colored Glazes	154-155
227. Parian Body Vases with Colored Glazes	
228. Parian Body Vases	158-159
229. Parian Body Vases with Applied Color	
230. Parian Porcelain Vases, Colored Decoration	
231. Blue and White Porcelain Vases with Gold Decoration	
232. Blue and White Porcelain Vases	160-161
233. Blue and White Porcelain Vases, Applied Decoration	
234. Unique Paul and Virginia Pattern Vase	162-163
235. Blue and White Porcelain Vases, Paul and Virginia Pattern	
236. Parian Porcelain Vases, Ear of Corn Design	
237. Blue and White Porcelain Vases, Ear of Corn Design	
238. Parian Porcelain Vases, Figures	164-165
239. Parian Porcelain Vases, Figures	
240. Parian Porcelain Vases, Hands	166-167
241. Parian Porcelain Vases, Hands	
242. Parian Porcelain Vases, Hands	168-169
243. Parian Porcelain Vases, Hands	
244. Parian Porcelain Vases	170-171
245. Parian Porcelain Vases	
246. Parian Porcelain Vases	172-173
247. Parian Porcelain Vases, Shell Motifs	
248. Parian Porcelain Vases	174-175
249. Parian Porcelain Vases	
250. Parian Porcelain Vases	176-177
251. Parian Porcelain Vases	
252. Parian Porcelain Vases, Applied Decoration	178-179
253. Comparison Pieces: Parian Vases, Grape-Decorated	
254. Parian Porcelain Vases and Cologne Bottle, Applied Decoration	
255. Parian Porcelain Vases, Applied Decoration	180-181
256. Parian Porcelain Vases, Applied Decoration	

	PAGE
257. Parian Porcelain Vases, Applied Decoration	182-183
258. Parian Porcelain Vases, Applied Decoration	
259. Parian Porcelain Vases	184-185
260. Parian Porcelain Vases, Applied Decoration	
261. Parian Porcelain Vases, Applied Decoration	186-187
262. Parian Porcelain Vases, Applied Decoration	
263. Parian Porcelain Vases	188-189
264. Parian Porcelain Vases	
265. Parian Porcelain Vases	190-191
266. Parian Porcelain Vases	
267. Parian Porcelain Vases	192-193
268. Parian Porcelain Vases, Applied Decoration	
269. Parian Porcelain Vases, Applied Decoration	194-195
270. Molded Vases with Applied Decoration	
271. Extremely Rare Footed Vases	196-197
272. Blue and White Porcelain Vases	
273. Two Rare Porcelain Vases, Swan Handles	198-199
274. Blue and White Porcelain Vases	
275. Blue and White Porcelain and Parian Vases	200-201
276. Blue and White Porcelain Vases	
277. Blue and White Porcelain Vases	202-203
278. Blue and White Porcelain Vases	
279. Blue and White Porcelain Vases, Poppy Pattern	204-205
280. Blue and White Porcelain Vases	
281. Blue and White Porcelain Vases	206-207
282. Blue and White Porcelain Vases	
283. Blue and Wihte Porcelain Vases	208-209
284. Blue and White Porcelain Vases	
285. Blue and White Porcelain Vases	210-211
286. Blue and White Porcelain Vases	
287. Blue and White Porcelain Vases	212-213
288. Blue and White Porcelain Vases	
289. Blue and White Porcelain Vases	214-215
290. Blue and White Porcelain Vases	
291. Blue and White Porcelain Vases	216-217
292. Blue and White Porcelain Vases	
293. Blue and White Porcelain Vases	218-219
294. Blue and White Porcelain Vases	
295. Exceptionally Fine Parian Porcelain Ewer	220-221
296. Two Rare Parian Porcelain Ewers	
297. Cologne Bottles and Ewer, Variations of the Same Design	
298. Parian Porcelain Ewers	222-223
299. Parian Porcelain Ewers	
300. Parian Porcelain Ewers	224-225
301. Parian Porcelain Vases and Ewer, Applied Decoration	
302. Parian Ewers, Applied Decoration	226-227
303. Parian Porcelain Ewers	
304. Blue and White Porcelain Ewer	228-229
305. Blue and White Porcelain Ewers	
306. Blue and White Porcelain Ewers	230-231
307. Blue and White Porcelain Ewers	
308. Blue and White Porcelain Ewers	232-233
309. Blue and White Porcelain Vases and Ewers	
310. Parian Cologne Bottles, Applied Flowers	234-235
311. Rare Cologne Bottles, Applied Grapes and Handles	
312. Parian Cologne Bottles	236-237
313. Parian Cologne Bottles	
314. Cologne Bottles, Applied Grapes	238-239
315. Cologne Bottles, Applied Decoration	
316. Three Covered Jars	

Halftone Plates (*continued*)   PAGE

317. Parian Trinket Boxes   240-241
318. Blue and White Porcelain Covered Jars
319. Covered Jars, Porcelain
320. Parian Trinket Boxes   242-243
321. Parian Trinket Boxes
322. Parian Trinket Boxes   244-245
323. Parian Trinket Boxes
324. Trinket Boxes, Assorted Materials   246-247
325. Parian and Blue and White Porcelain Trinket Boxes
326. Blue and White Porcelain Trinket Boxes   248-249
327. Blue and White Porcelain Trinket Boxes
328. Blue and White Porcelain Trinket Boxes   250-251
329. Blue and White Porcelain Trinket Boxes
330. Trinket Boxes with Cherubs on Top   252-253
331. Blue and White Porcelain Trinket Boxes
332. Trinket Boxes with Animals on Top   254-255
333. Blue and White Porcelain Trinket Box
334. Rare Parian Statuette   257
335. Extremely Rare Parian Bust   258-259
336. Parian Busts
337. Rare Parian Statuette   260-261
338. Rare Parian Statuette
339. Parian Statuettes
340. Parian Statuette   262-263
341. Rare Parian Statuette
342. Parian Statuettes
343. Pair of Rare Parian Statuettes   264-265
344. Pair of Parian Statuettes
345. Parian Angel   266-267
346. Parian Statuette
347. Rare Parian Statuette
348. Three Rare Statuettes   268-269
349. Parian Statuettes
350. Parian Statuettes
351. Parian Statuettes   270-271
352. Parian Statuettes
353. Parian Statuettes   272-273
354. Parian Statuettes and Two Whistles
355. Two Extremely Rare Statuettes   274-275
356. Parian Statuettes
357. Parian Statuettes   276-277
358. Parian Statuettes
359. Parian Statuettes
360. Graniteware Statuette   278-279
361. Parian Statuettes
362. Parian Statuettes
363. Parian Statuette of a Ewe   281
364. Flint Enamel Stag   282-283
365. Flint Enamel Stag
366. Two Pairs of Recumbent Deer   284-285
367. A Kennel of Poodles
368. Pair of Rockingham Poodles   286-287
369. Pair of Flint Enamel Poodles
370. Extremely Rare Pair of Glazed Yellowware Poodles
371. Rare Parian Poodle   288-289
372. Rare Parian Poodle

373. Extremely Rare Graniteware Poodle   290-291
374. Extremely Rare Pair of Graniteware Poodles
375. Extremely Rare Light Green Mottled Flint Enamel Lion   292-293
376. Flint Enamel Lion
377. A Den of Flint Enamel Lions
378. A Dairy of Cows   294-295
379. Extremely Rare Flint Enamel Recumbent Cow
380. Flint Enamel Recumbent Cow
381. Flint Enamel Cow Creamers   296-297
382. Two Extremely Rare Cow Creamers
383. Two Extremely Rare Cow Creamers
384. Only Known Scroddled Ware Cow Creamer
385. Parian Ornaments, with Horses and Cows   298-299
386. Parian Vases and Ornaments with Animals
387. Small Parian Ornaments with Sheep
388. Parian Ornaments with Animals
389. Parian Greyhound Ornaments   300-301
390. Extremely Rare Porcelain Ornaments with Cats
391. Parian Ornaments and Vases with Dogs
392. Hanging Parian Bird Ornament   302-303
393. Parian Vases with Birds
394. Small Parian Ornaments with Geese, Partridge
395. Small Parian Vases with Frogs, Chicks
396. Parian Ornaments and Vases with Swans   304-305
397. Extremely Rare Graniteware Swan
398. Extremely Rare Smear-Glazed Swan
399. Eagle Forms, Various Items   306-307
400. Rare Parian Eagle Vases
401. Eagle Vases
402. Only Known Example Yellowware Toby Snuff Jar   309
403. Extremely Rare Stoneware Inkstand   310-311
404. Comparison Pieces: Greyhound Inkwells
405. Rare Graniteware Inkwell, Phrenological Head
406. Rockingham and Flint Enamel Inkwells   312-313
407. Flint Enamel Paperweights
408. Graniteware Paperweights
409 and 409A. Extremely Rare Rockingham Desk Set   314-315
410. Marked Scroddled Ware Book Flask
411. Book Flasks   316-317
412. Rockingham Boots and Shoes
413. Novelty Flint Enamel Clenched Fist
414. Extremely Rare Graniteware Hand Dish
415. Extremely Rare Scroddled Ware Toby Pitcher   318-319
416 and 416A. Toby Pitchers
417. Rare Toby Snuff Jars   320-321
418. Toby Snuff Jars
419. Rare Toby Bottles, Three Sizes
420. Only Known Examples Toby Items   322-323
421. Rare Toby Bottles
422. Extremely Rare Toby Barrel Bottles

423. Only Known Example Graniteware Toby Bottle
424. Flint Enamel Covered Toby Head   324-325
425. Flint Enamel Zachary Taylor Pitchers
426. Extremely Rare Flint Enamel Swiss Lady
427. Only Known Example Flint Enamel Swiss Lady Bank
428. Banks   326-327
429. Banks
430. Blue and White Porcelain Fragments of a Head
431. Only Known Example Blue and White Porcelain Pipe
432. Extremely Rare Parian Basket of Flowers   328-329
433. John Harrison's Baskets with Applied Flowers
434. Extremely Rare Parian Miniature Baskets of Applied Flowers
435. Rare Parian Basket with Applied Flowers   330-331
436. Rare Parian Baskets with Applied Decoration
437. Rare Parian Jewelry with Applied Flowers
438. Rare Parian Sewing Accessories   332-333
439. Parian Novelty Items
440. Extremely Rare Majolica-Type and Parian Items   334-335
441. Miniature Parian Porcelain Pitchers
442. Miniature Parian Porcelain Pitchers   336-337
443. Miniature Parian Vases and Pitchers
444. Miniature Blue and White Porcelain Pitchers   338-339
445. Miniature Blue and White Porcelain Vases
446. Rare Parian Toy Tea Set   340-341
447. Rare Common White Pottery Tea Set
448. Only Known Example Brown Slip-Covered Toy Dishes
449. Miniature Stoneware Crocks, Cobalt-Decorated   342
450. Miniature Rockingham and Flint Enamel Items

Figures   PAGE

I. Price List of Norton Pottery   9
II. Price List from Norton & Fenton Pottery
III. Price List of Fenton's Pottery   10
IV. Illustrated Price List of J. & E. Norton Pottery   11
V. Price List of E. & L. P. Norton Pottery
VI. Norton Potters   12
VII. Catalogue Pages from Edward Norton & Co. Pottery
VIII. Bennington Leaders in Flint Enamel and Rockingham Picture Frames   13
IX. Marks Used by Fenton on Flint Enamel Ware   14
X. Marks Used by Fenton and His Pottery
XI. Woodcut Illustration of Crystal Palace Exhibit   15
XII. Plaster Models for Making Molds   20

INDEX OF ILLUSTRATIONS

A

Alcock, Samuel, 50
alphabet letters, 139
animals (see animal desired, i.e. cow, deer, lion, sheep, etc.)

B

baking dishes
  flint enamel, 106
  Rockingham, 106
Ballard Bros., 32
banks (see also toby banks)
  brown slip-covered, 326
  flint enamel, 325-26
  Rockingham, 326
  stoneware, 111
baskets of flowers, 18, 328-30
Bates, William, 12
beakers, 96
bean pots (see pipkins)
bedpans, 123
Belleek-type ware
  trinket boxes, 246
  vases, 153, 307
Bennett Bros., 97
birds, 302-03
bird in nest, 333
blue porcelain
  sugar bowl, 84
  teapot, 84
blue and white porcelain
  bowl, covered, 87
  cane head, 327
  cologne bottles. 221, 235, 238-39
  ewers, 188E, 228-32
  ornaments, 300
  pipe, 327
  pitchers, 41-42, 45-46, 51, 58, 62, 74-75, 87, 188D, 338
  plates, 88
  spill-holders, 144
  statuettes, 268
  trinket boxes, 188D, 239-41, 246-55
  vases, 144, 148-51, 159, 160-63, 188A, 195-219, 233, 339
book bottles (see book flasks)
book flasks
  brown slip-covered, 316
  flint enamel, 316
  Rockingham, 316
  scroddled ware, 315
boots
  Parian, 333
  Rockingham, 316
bottles (see also book flasks; cologne bottles)
  flint enamel, 93, 188A
  stoneware, 110
bowls (see also baking dishes; miniatures)
  flint enamel, 105
  Parian, 88-89
  Rockingham, 107, 125
  stoneware, 6, 111
  yellowware, 108
bowls, covered, 87, 92
boxes, covered (see trinket boxes)
bracelets (see jewelry)
brooches (see jewelry)
brown and white porcelain
  pitchers, 76
  trinket boxes, 250
brown slip-covered
  banks, 326
  book flasks, 316
  jardinieres, 12
  jug, 3
  pitcher, 54
  shaving mug, 103
  stoneware (see stoneware, item desired, i.e. banks, jars, mugs, etc.)
  toby bottles, 321-322
  toby snuff jars, 320
  toy dishes, 341
buck (see deer)
busts, Parian (see Parian, statuettes)
butter dish
  flint enamel, 93
Burlington, Vt., 32-33
Burt, Gilbert F., 12

C

Caire, J. B. & Co., 33
cake molds
  flint enamel, 105
  Rockingham, 105
cake plate (see plate, cake)
candleholders (see candlesticks)
candle snuffer, 333
candlesticks
  flint enamel, 134-35
  Rockingham, 134-35

cane head, 327
cats, 300
chamber pots
  flint enamel, 123
  graniteware, 123
change cover
  flint enamel, 188A, 320, 322, 325
chicks, 303
churns, 110
Clark, Decius, 291
Clark, L. W. Co., 72
clock case, Parian, 18
coachman (see toby bottles)
Cobridge, England, 47
coffeepot
  flint enamel, 98
  glazed white porcelain, 91
coffee urn, flint enamel, 83
cologne bottles
  blue and white porcelain, 221, 235, 238-39
  Parian, 143, 179, 221, 234-39
colored glazes on porcelain,
  pitchers, 23, 188A
  plates, 88
  trinket boxes, 251
  vases, 149, 154-58, 306
common white toy tea set, 340
compotes (see also fruit baskets)
  Parian, 88
cooler, water (see water cooler)
Copeland, 61, 129, 261
covered bowl (see bowl, covered)
covered boxes (see trinket boxes)
covered butter dish (see butter dish)
covered jars (see jars, covered)
covered toddy cups (see cups)
cows (see also cow creamers), 255, 298
  flint enamel, 295
  Rockingham, 294
cow creamers
  flint enamel, 296
  graniteware, 188A, 296-97
  identification points, 296
  scroddled ware, 297
  yellowware, 188A, 296
creamers (see also pitchers)
  flint enamel, 98
  Parian, 85-86
crocks (see also miniatures)
  stoneware, 5, 7
croup kettle, Rockingham, 113
crosses (see jewelry)
cups (see also miniatures)
  glazed white porcelain, 90-91
  graniteware, 38
  Parian, 88
cups, custard (see bowls)
curtain tie-backs (see tie-backs)
cuspidors (see also miniatures)
  flint enamel, 128-129
  Rockingham, 128
  scroddled ware, 129
  stoneware, 110
custard cups (see bowls)

D

dark luster, 24-25, 188F
darning egg, Parian, 333
desk set, Rockingham, 314
deer,
  flint enamel, 17, 282-84
  Parian, 284, 298
doe (see deer)
dogs (see greyhounds; ornaments; paperweights; pitchers, hound-handled; poodles)
door knobs
  flint enamel, 136
  Rockingham, 136
door knob escutcheons, graniteware, 137
drawer pulls
  flint enamel, 136
  Rockingham, 136
dresser sets (see cologne bottles)

E

eagle forms and designs, 306-07
East Liverpool, Ohio, 32, 106, 129
earrings (see jewelry)
egg cup, Parian, 89
escutcheons (see also name plates)
  graniteware, 137
Etruria Works, 129
ewe (see sheep)
ewers (see also pitchers; vases)
  blue and white porcelain, 188D, 188E, 228-32
  Parian, 220-27

F

Fenton, Christopher Webber, portrait of, 13

figure of lady (see change cover)
fist, flint enamel, 317
Fitz-Cook, Henry, 66-67
flasks (see book flasks)
flint enamel
  baking dishes, 106
  banks, 325-26
  bedpans, 123
  book flasks, 316
  bottles, 93, 188A
  bowls, 105
  butter dish, 93
  cake molds, 105
  candlesticks, 134-35
  chamber pots, 123
  change covers, 320, 322, 325
  coffeepot, 98
  coffee urn, 83
  cows, 295
  cow creamers, 296
  creamer, 98
  cuspidors, 128-29
  deer, 17, 282-84
  door knobs, 136
  drawer pulls, 136
  fist, 317
  foot baths, 126
  foot warmers, 127
  inkwells, 312
  jardinieres, 130
  lamp bases, 140-41, 188C
  lions, 188A, 292-293
  name plates, 138
  paperweights, 312
  picture frames, 13, 138
  pie plate, 106
  pipkins, 104
  pitchers, 26-29, 48, 52, 98, 101, 319, 324
  poodles, 285-86
  relish dish, 93
  scroll supports, 132
  slop jars, 125
  soap dishes, 116-17
  spill-holders, 282-84, 295
  statuettes, 274
  sugar bowls, 93, 98
  teapots, 98-99
  tie-backs, 136
  tiles, 133
  tobacco jars, 94-95
  toby banks, 321
  toby bottles, 188F, 321-23
  toby head, 324
  toby pitchers, 319, 324
  toby snuff jars, 320-21
  toilet boxes, 116-17
  vases, 145-47
  washbasin, 112
  washbowl and pitcher sets, 118-19, 188B
  water cooler, 114, 117
flower baskets (see baskets of flowers)
flower pots (see also jardinieres)
  brown slip-covered, 131
flowers, Parian, 18
foot baths
  flint enamel, 126
  graniteware, 126
foot warmers
  flint enamel, 127
  graniteware, 127
  Rockingham, 127
fox, 298-99
frames (see picture frames)
frogs, 303
fruit basket, graniteware, 90

G

glasses (see beakers)
glazed white porcelain
  coffeepot, 91
  cups, 90-91
  pitchers, 23, 40, 70, 73-74, 77, 79, 81, 91, 334
  plate, cake, 91
  saucers, 90-91
  sugar bowl, 91
  teapot, 91
goblets (see also miniatures)
  Rockingham, 96-97
Godfrey, Frederick, 12
goose, 303
graniteware
  chamber pots, 123
  cow creamers, 296-97
  cup, 38
  doorknob escutcheon, 137
  escutcheons, 137
  foot baths, 126

foot warmers, 127
fruit basket, 90
hand dish, 317
inkwell, 311
keyhole covers, 137
name plates, 137
ornaments, 305
paperweights, 306, 313
pitchers, 35, 37-39, 41, 46, 48, 51-52, 55, 62, 68, 77
poodles, 285, 290-91
shaving mugs, 115
slop jars, 124
soap dishes, 116
spill-holders, 144
statuettes, 278
tie-backs, 137
toby bottles, 323
toilet sets, 122
vases, 144, 147
washbowl and pitcher sets, 121-22
whistles, 273
gray-green porcelain
pitchers, 59
Greatbach, Daniel, 17
green and white porcelain
vases, 152
Greenpoint, N. J., 39
Greenslet, Frank H., 12
greyhounds
Parian, 300, 310
stoneware, 188F, 310

H

hair container (see trinket boxes)
hands, Parian, 333
hand dish, graniteware, 317
Harrison, John, 246, 328, 340
hen, 302
horses, 298-99
Houghwout & Co., 39
hound-handled pitchers (see pitchers, hound-handled)

I

identification (see marks)
inhalators (see croup kettle)
ink bottle, stoneware, 110
ink stands (see inkwells)
inkwells (see also desk set)
flint enamel, 312
graniteware, 311
Parian, 89, 273
Rockingham, 312
stoneware, 188F, 310

J

jars (see also slop jars; tobacco jars)
stoneware, 4, 110
jars, covered, 239-41
jars, snuff (see toby snuff jars)
jardinieres (see also miniatures)
brown slip-covered, 12
flint enamel, 130
Rockingham, 130-31
jewel box (see trinket boxes)
jewelry, Parian, 331
Johnson, Jerome, 12
Jones & Walley, 47, 50
jugs (see also miniatures)
brown slip-covered, 3
red earthenware, 3
stoneware, 5-8, 110-11

K

keyholes (see escutcheons; keyhole covers)
keyhole covers
graniteware, 137
Parian, 139
Kimball, Charles C., 12

L

lamp bases
flint enamel, 140-41, 188C
latticework bowls, Parian, 330
Leake, William, 13, 316
letters, alphabet, 139
lions,
flint enamel, 188A, 292-93

M

majolica-type earthenware,
catalogue pages, 12
pitcher, 334
vase, 334
marks,
Fenton's Works, 14
flint enamel 1849, 14
in gold leaf, 149
Norton & Fenton, 24-25
Norton & Fenton, stoneware, 13
U. S. Pottery, 14
Mayer, T. J. and J., 56-57, 88
Meigh, Charles and Sons, 195
Metz, Jacob, 12
miniatures (see also baskets of flowers)
bowl, 342

crocks, 342
cup, 342
cuspidor, 342
goblet, 342
jardiniere, 342
jugs, 342
pitchers, 110, 335-36, 338, 342
saucer, 342
vases, 148, 337, 339
mixing bowls (see bowls)
models, plaster, 20
molds (see cake molds)
monk bottles (see toby bottles)
monument at Crystal Palace, 16
Moore, Edward H., 12
mortar ware, 109
mortars and pestles, 109
mugs (see also shaving mugs)
Rockingham, 97
stoneware, 111
mustard pot, Parian, 87, 89

N

name plates,
flint enamel, 138
graniteware, 137
Parian, 139
Rockingham, 138
nappies (see bowls)
Nichols & Alford, 33
Norton & Fenton marks, 13, 24-25
Norton
Captain John, 3-4
Edward, 12-13
John H., 12
Julius, 13, 328
Luman, 13
novelty items, 317

O

ornaments (see also jewelry; novelty items)
blue and white porcelain, 300
graniteware, 305
Parian, 281, 298-304, 306
smear glaze, 305

P

paperweights
flint enamel, 312
graniteware, 306, 313
Parian (see also smear glaze porcelain)
bird in nest, 333
boots, 333
bowl, 88-89
busts (see Parian, statuettes)
candle snuffer, 333
clock case, 18
cologne bottles, 143, 179, 221, 234-39
compotes, 88
creamers, 85-86
cups, 88
darning egg, 333
deer, 284, 298
egg cup, 89
ewers, 220-27
flowers, 18
greyhounds, 300, 310
hands, 333
inkwells, 89, 273
jewelry, 331
keyhole covers, 139
latticework bowls, 330
mustard pots, 87, 89
name plates, 139
ornaments (see also novelty items), 281, 298-304, 306
pincushions, 332
pinholders, 332
pitchers, 23, 40-43, 45-46, 50-51, 53, 62-63, 65-66, 70-72, 76-79, 80-81, 85-86, 89, 334-36
plates, 87
poodles, 188A, 285, 288-89
salt shaker, 89
saucers, 88
spill-holders, 262, 270-72
statuettes, 16, 257, 259-69, 271-73, 275, 279
sugar bowls, 84-86, 89
teapots, 84-85
tie-backs, 137
toothpick holder, 89
toy tea set, 340
trinket boxes, 239-47, 251-52, 254
vases, 148, 150-52, 156, 158, 160, 163-95, 188D, 198, 200, 225, 298-99, 301-04, 306-07, 334, 337
whistles, 273
Park, Calvin, 13
parrot, 302
partridge, 303
peacock, 302
pendants (see jewelry)
perfume bottle (see cologne bottles)

pestles and mortar, 109
pie plates
flint enamel, 106
Rockingham, 106
picture frames
flint enamel, 13, 138
Rockingham, 13
pin boxes (see trinket boxes)
pincushions, 332
pinholders, 332
pink and white porcelain
pitchers, 45
plates, 88
vases, 152
pink glazed porcelain, 239, 300
pipe, blue and white porcelain, 327
pipkins
flint enamel, 104
Rockingham, 104
yellowware, 104
pitchers (see also cow creamers; creamers; ewers; miniatures; toby pitchers; toilet sets; washbowl and pitcher sets)
Alternate Rib pattern, 26, 101
Apostle pattern, 74
Babes in the Woods pattern, 75
barrel-shaped, 28
Bird and Nest pattern, 76, 78
blue and white porcelain, 41-42, 45-46, 49, 51, 58, 62, 74-75, 87, 188D, 338
brown and white porcelain, 76
brown glazed porcelain, 76
brown slip-covered, 54
Cascade pattern, 40
Charter Oak pattern, 41
Cherub and Grapes pattern, 42, 188D
Climbing Ivy pattern, 77-78
colored bands, 35
colored glazes on porcelain, 23, 188A
Corn Husk pattern, 43
cream buff porcelain bisque, 72
Cupid and Psyche pattern, 44-45, 79
Daffodil pattern, 46, 79
dark luster, 24-25
Day and Night pattern, 74
Diamond pattern, 26, 29
dog-handled (see pitchers, hound-handled)
Fern pattern, 77
flint enamel, 26-29, 48, 52, 98, 101, 188B, 319, 324
Geometric Arabesque pattern, 46, 81
glazed white porcelain, 23, 40, 70, 73-74, 77, 79, 81, 91, 334
Good Samaritan pattern, 47
Gothic pattern, 28
graniteware, 35, 37-39, 41, 46, 48, 51-52, 55, 62, 68, 77
gray-green porcelain, 59
Gypsy pattern (see pitchers, Good Samaritan pattern)
hound-handled, 30-33
hunting scene, 27
Ivy pattern, 74
Ivy-vine pattern, 48
Lily Pad pattern, 49, 78
Love and War pattern, 50
majolica-type earthenware, 334
Mask pattern, 75
mask lip, 27, 46
miniatures, 110, 335-36, 338
Palm Tree pattern, 76-77, 188A
Paneled Acanthus Leaf pattern, 52
Paneled Grapevine pattern, 51-52
Paneled Vine and Flower pattern, 53
Parian, 23, 40-43, 45-46, 50-51, 53, 62-63, 65-66, 70-72, 76-79, 80-81, 85-86, 89, 334-36
Paul and Virginia pattern, 54-55, 58-59, 75, 77
pink and white porcelain, 45
Pond Lily pattern, 59-60, 62-64
Pond Lily and Acanthus Leaf pattern, 65
Presentation pattern, 36-39, 188A
Rockingham, 24-33, 36, 44, 52, 64
Scalloped Rib pattern, 27
scroddled ware, 29, 34
Sheaf of Wheat pattern, 77
Shell pattern, 336
smear glaze, 47, 53, 79
Snowdrop pattern, 66
Spinning Wheel pattern, 74, 78
stoneware, 5, 110-11
swan-neck handle, 74
Sweetheart (see pitchers, Presentation pattern)
tan and white porcelain, 188A
Tulip and Heart pattern, 26
Tulip and Sunflower pattern, 68, 70-72, 87
Wheat in Panel pattern, 74
Wild Rose pattern, 23, 72-73, 188A

347

plaster models, 20
plates
  blue and white porcelain, 88
  colored glazes on porcelain, 88
  glazed white porcelain, 90
  Parian, 87
  pink and white porcelain, 88
  Rockingham, 106
Po'keepsie, N. Y., 33
poodles
  flint enamel, 285-86
  graniteware, 285, 290-91
  Parian, 188A, 285, 288-89
  Rockingham, 188A, 285-86
  yellowware, 285, 287
Portugal, 72
Powers, Hiram, 261
price lists, 9-12

R

ram (see sheep)
red earthenware, 3-4, 36
recumbent cow (see cow)
recumbent deer (see deer)
relish dish, flint enamel, 93
Rockingham
  baking dishes, 106
  banks, 326
  beakers, 96
  book flasks, 316
  boots, 316
  bowls, 107, 125
  cake molds, 105
  candlesticks, 134-35
  covered bowl, 92
  cow, 294
  croup kettle, 113
  cuspidors, 128
  desk set, 314
  door knobs, 136
  drawer pulls, 136
  foot warmer, 127
  goblets, 96-97
  hound-handled pitchers, 33
  inkwells, 312
  jardinieres, 130-31
  mugs, 97
  name plates, 138
  picture frames, 13
  pie plate, 106
  pipkins, 104
  pitchers, 24-33, 36, 44, 52, 64
  plates, 106
  poodles, 188A, 285-86
  shoes, 316
  slop jars, 125
  soap dishes, 116
  statuettes, 274
  teapots, 99-100
  tie-backs, 136
  tiles, 133
  tobacco jars, 94-95
  toby bottles, 188F, 321-23
  toby pitchers, 319
  toilet boxes, 116
  vases, 145
  washboard, 112
  water cooler, 115
rooster, 302

S

salt shaker, Parian, 89
saucers (see also miniatures)
  glazed white porcelain, 90-91
  Parian, 88
scroddled ware
  book flask, 315
  cow creamer, 297
  cuspidor, 129
  pitchers, 29, 34
  slop jar, 124
  toby jug, 188A
  toby pitchers, 318
  vases, 147
  washbowl and pitcher set, 120
scroll supports, 132
shaving mugs
  brown slip-covered, 103
  graniteware, 115
sheep, 281, 299
shelf brackets, 132
shoes, Rockingham, 316
slop jars
  flint enamel, 125
  graniteware, 124
  Rockingham, 125
  scroddled ware, 124
smear glaze
  ornaments, 305
  pitchers, 47, 53, 79
Smith, William, 12
snuff jars (see toby snuff jars)

soap dishes
  flint enamel, 116-17
  graniteware, 116
  Rockingham, 116
sparrow, 303
spill-holders (see also vases)
  blue and white porcelain, 144
  flint enamel, 282-84, 295
  graniteware, 144
  Parian, 262, 270-72
stag (see deer)
standing stag (see deer)
statuettes
  angel, 266
  "Autumn," 260
  baby on couch, 269; in cradle, 269
  baby resting on basket, 273
  Bacchus, 266
  blue and white porcelain, 268
  boy with: basket, 264; bird, 263; book, 265;
    dog, 263; egg basket, 271; tricorne hat,
    262
  busts, 258-59
  child in chair, 268
  child with laurel wreath, 272
  cherub, 267
  classic figure, 270
  eagle and baby, 273
  "Egypt, Romans, Greece," 261
  fisherman with basket, 271
  flint enamel, 274
  frowning girl with marbles, 271
  girl with: book, 265; dog, 263; harp, 277;
    hat, 264; lyre, 276-77; nesting bird, 262
  goat, 270
  graniteware, 278
  "Greek Slave, The," 261
  hunter with gun, 271
  kneeling child with rabbit, 269
  man with faggots, 271
  Milton, 271
  monkey with dog, 270
  Parian, 16, 257, 259-69, 271-73, 275, 279
  praying: angel, 268; child, 268, 278; girl,
    268, 279; girl with book, 276-77; Samuel,
    16, 188A, 279
  Red Riding Hood, 273-75
  Rockingham, 274
  seated girl, 260
  "Simply to Thy Cross I Cling," 257
  sitting boy, 270
  sleeping: boy, 268; child, 268, 279
  "Tight Shoe, The," 188A, 275
stoneware
  banks, 111
  bottles, 110
  bowls, 6, 111
  churns, 110
  crocks, 5, 7
  cuspidor, 110
  greyhounds, 310
  ink bottle, 110
  inkwell, 188F, 310
  jars, 4, 110
  jugs, 5-8, 110-11
  mugs, 111
  pitchers, 5, 110-11
  stovepipe liners, 110
  toby bottles, 188F, 322
  water cooler, 7
stovepipe liner, stoneware, 110
sugar bowls
  blue porcelain, 84
  flint enamel, 93, 98
  glazed white porcelain, 91
  Parian, 84-86, 89
swans, 304-05
Swiss Lady (see banks; change covers)

T

tan and white porcelain, 188A
teapots
  blue porcelain, 84
  flint enamel, 98-99
  glazed white porcelain, 91
  Parian, 84-85
  Rockingham, 99-100
tie-backs
  flint enamel, 136
  graniteware, 137
  Parian, 137
  Rockingham, 136
tiles
  flint enamel, 133
  Rockingham, 133
Tiltonville, Ohio, 33
tobacco jars
  flint enamel, 94-95
  Rockingham, 94-95
toby banks, flint enamel, 321
toby barrel bottles (see toby bottles)

toby bottles
  brown slip-covered, 321-22
  flint enamel, 188F, 321-23
  graniteware, 323
  Rockingham, 188F, 321, 323
  stoneware, 188A, 322
toby head, flint enamel, 324
toby jug, frontispiece
toby pitchers
  flint enamel, 319, 324
  Rockingham, 319
  scroddled ware, 188A, 318
toby snuff jars
  brown slip-covered, 320
  flint enamel, 320-21
  yellowware, 319
toilet boxes
  flint enamel, 116-17
  Rockingham, 116
toilet sets, graniteware, 122
toilet water bottles (see cologne bottles)
toothpick holder, Parian, 89
toy tea sets
  brown slip-covered, 341
  common white, 340
  Parian, 340
toys (see miniatures)
trinket boxes
  blue and white porcelain, 188D, 239-41,
    246-55
  colored glazes on porcelain, 251
  Parian, 239-47, 251-52, 254
Turk's head cake mold (see cake mold)

U

U. S. Pottery, drawing of, 13
urn, coffee, (see coffee urn)

V

Vance Faience Co., 33
vases, (see also ewers; spill-holders)
  acorns, 170
  Belleek-type, 153, 307
  blue and white porcelain, 144, 148-51, 160-
    63, 188A, 195-219, 233, 339, with gold
    decoration, 159-60
  colored glazes on porcelain, 149, 154-58,
    306
  cottage-type, 147, 149, 188A
  crocus, 170
  Ear of Corn pattern, 163, 216
  figures, Parian, 164-65
  flint enamel, 145-47
  graniteware, 144, 147
  green and white porcelain, 152
  hands, 166-69, with shell, 169
  Holly pattern, 189
  Lily of the Valley pattern, 189, 216
  majolica-type, 334
  miniatures, 148, 337, 339
  Parian, 148, 150-52, 156, 158, 160, 163-
    95, 188D, 198, 200, 225, 298-99, 301-04,
    306-07, 334
  Paul and Virginia pattern, 162
  pink and white porcelain, 152
  Poppy pattern, 204
  portrait medallion, Victoria and Albert,
    150-51
  red earthenware, 3
  Rockingham, 145
  scroddled ware, 147
  Shell motifs, 173
  Songbird pattern, 205
  swan handle, 198
  tulip-shaped, 146-47

W

Walley, Smith and Skinner, 310, 316A
washbasin, flint enamel, 112
washboard, Rockingham, 112
washbowl and pitcher sets
  flint enamel, 118-19, 188B
  graniteware, 121-22
  scroddled ware, 120
water coolers
  flint enamel, 17, 114
  Rockingham, 115
  stoneware, 7
Wedgwood Co., 42
"Wedgwood ware," 109
West Sterling, Mass., 310
whistles
  graniteware, 273
  Parian, 273
Williams, J. A. N., 12

Y

yellowware
  bowls, 108
  cow creamers, 296
  pipkins, 104
  poodles, 285, 287
  toby snuff jar, 319

Z

Zachary Taylor pitcher, 324